May imagination soar high and colors come to life as you explore the wonderful realm of dragons. May each stroke be an adventure and each color a unique magic. May this book bring joy and creativity to your world, filling it with fantasy and fun.
With affection,


Felipe Silva

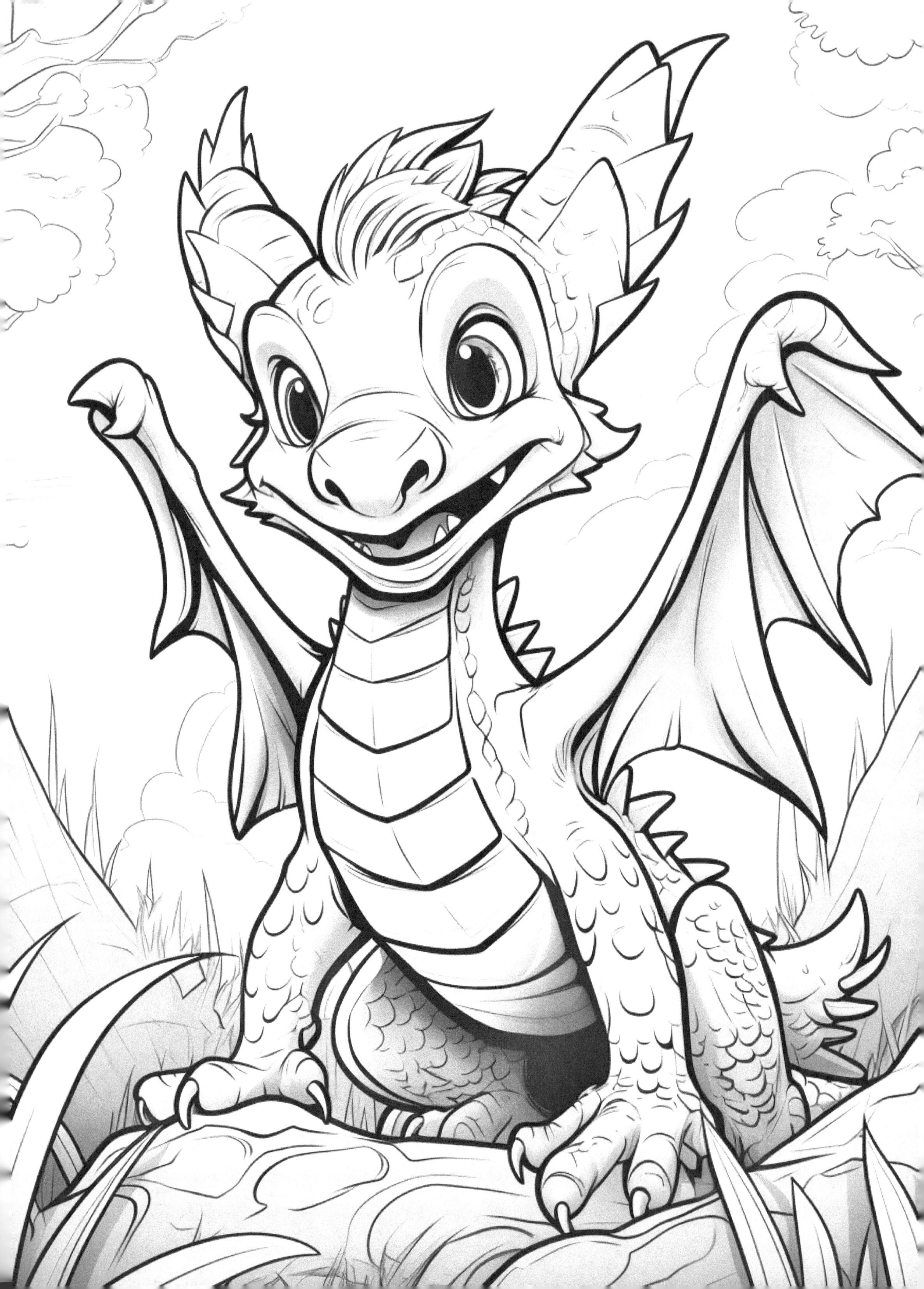

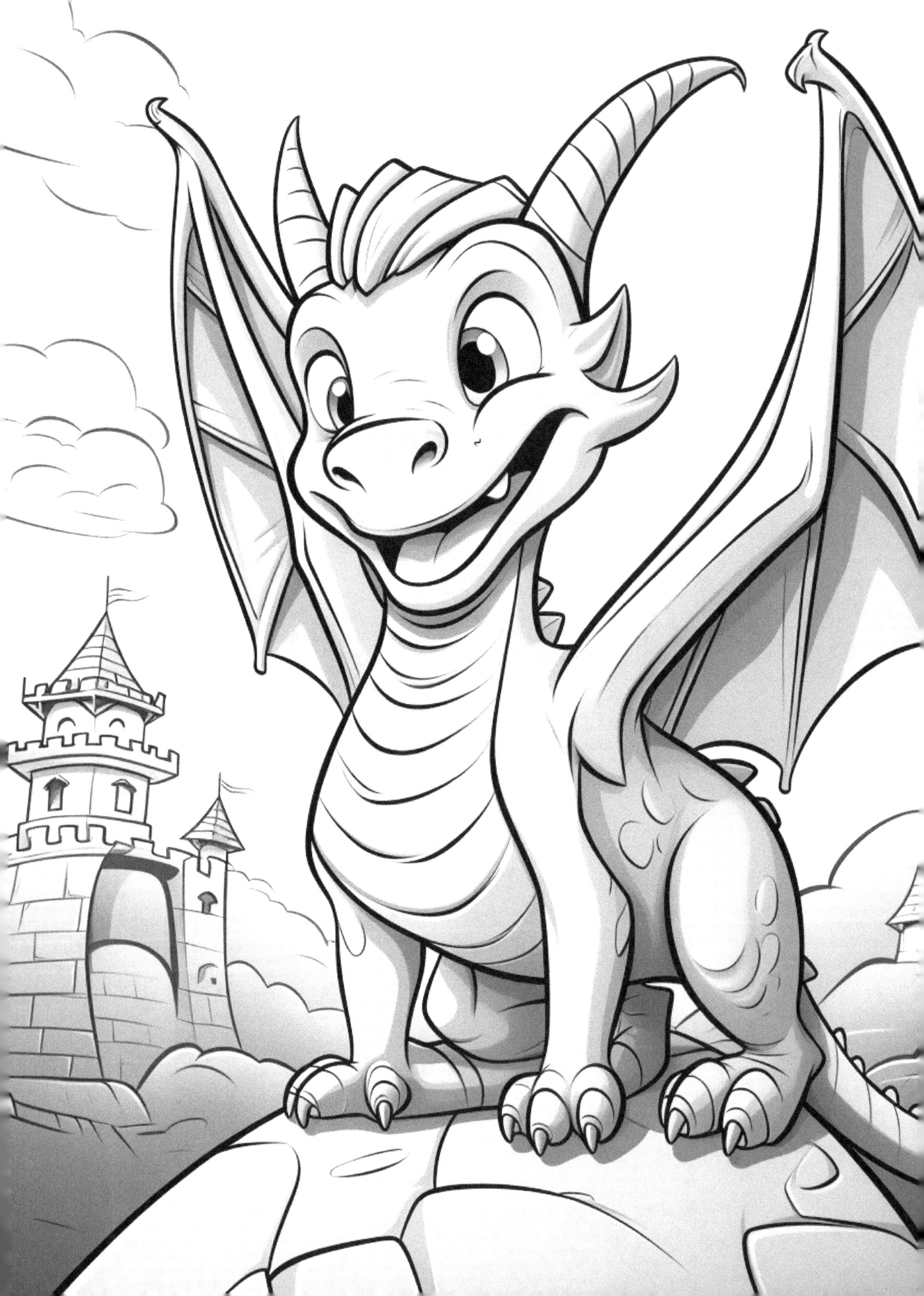

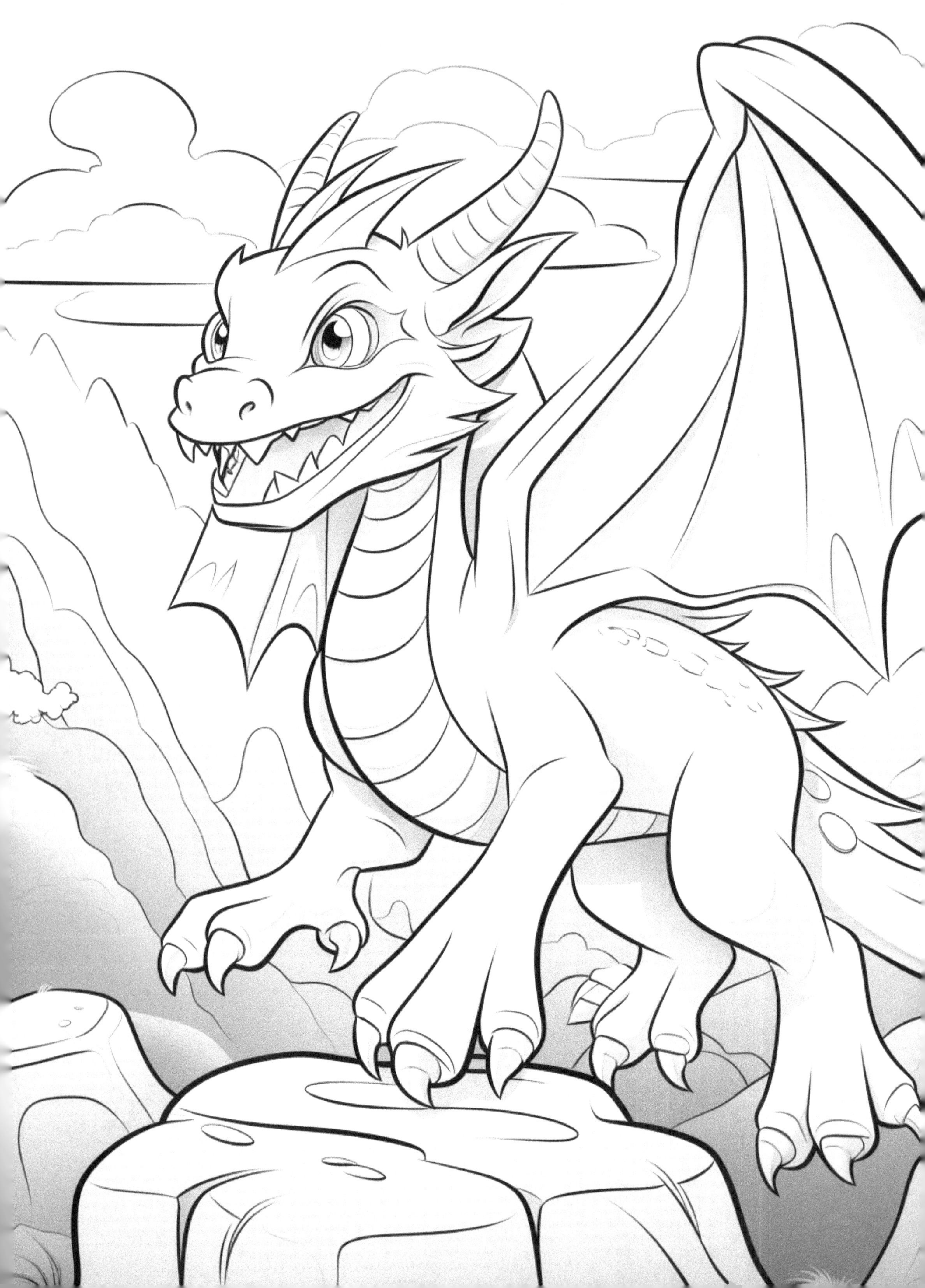

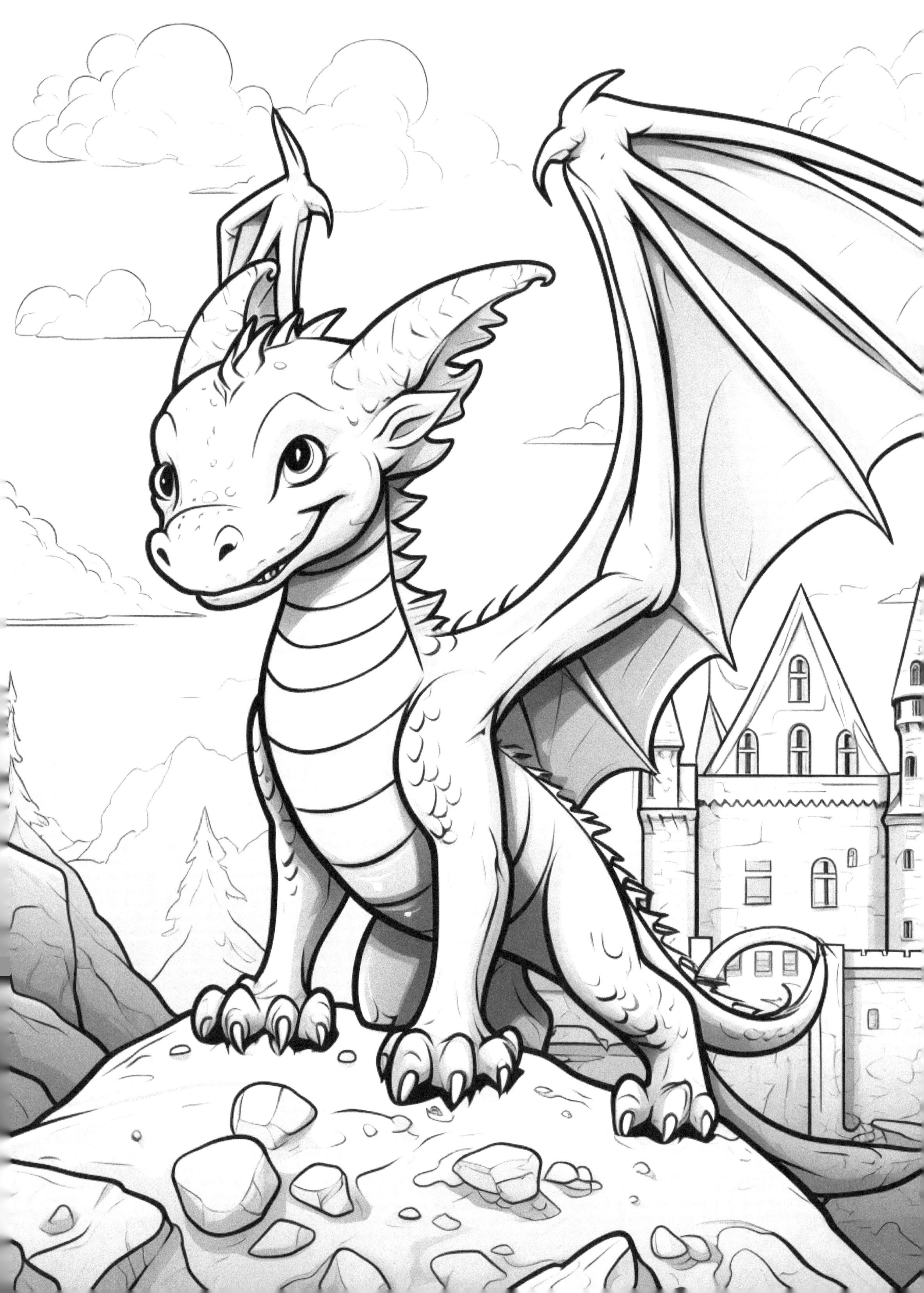

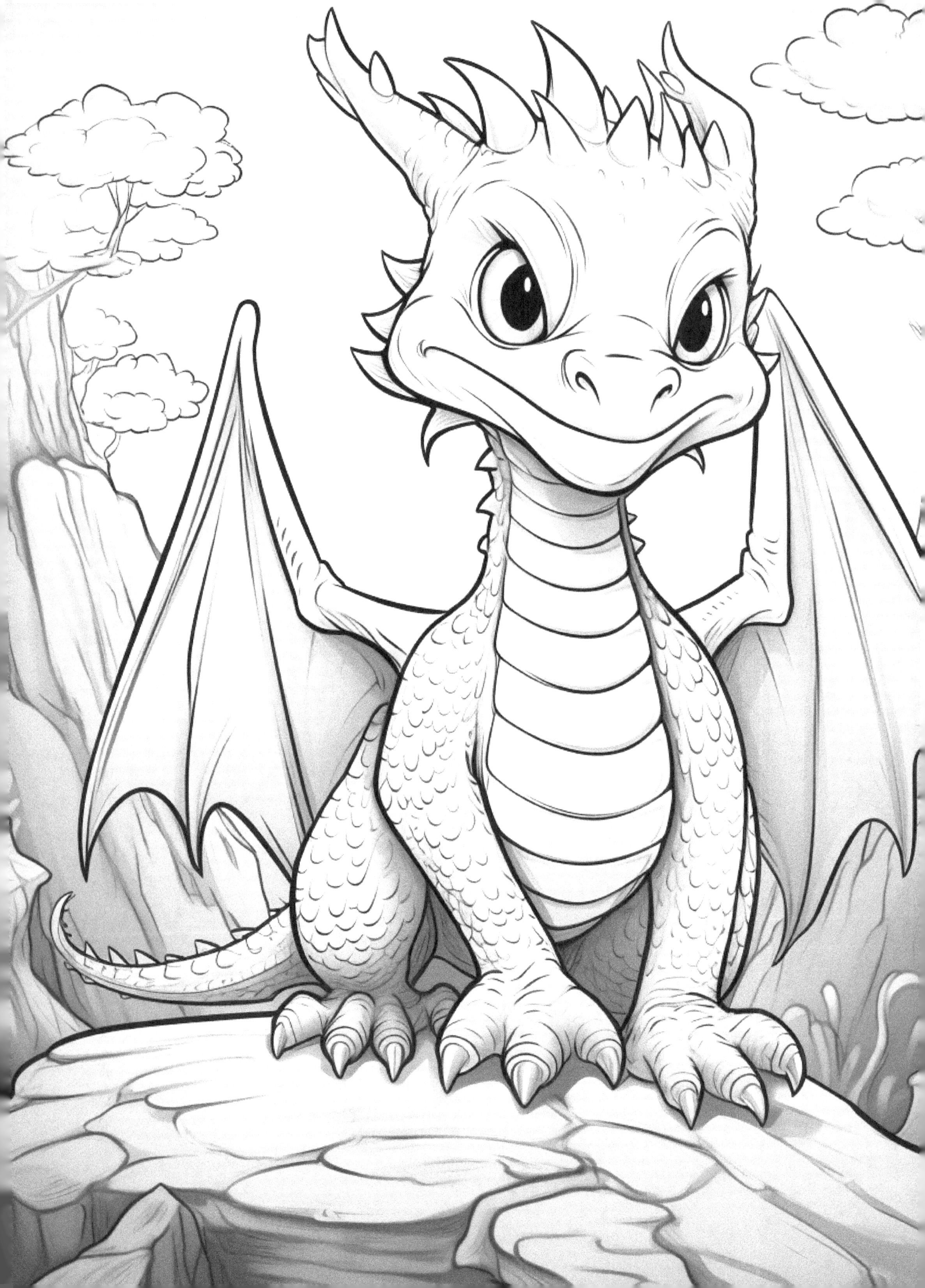

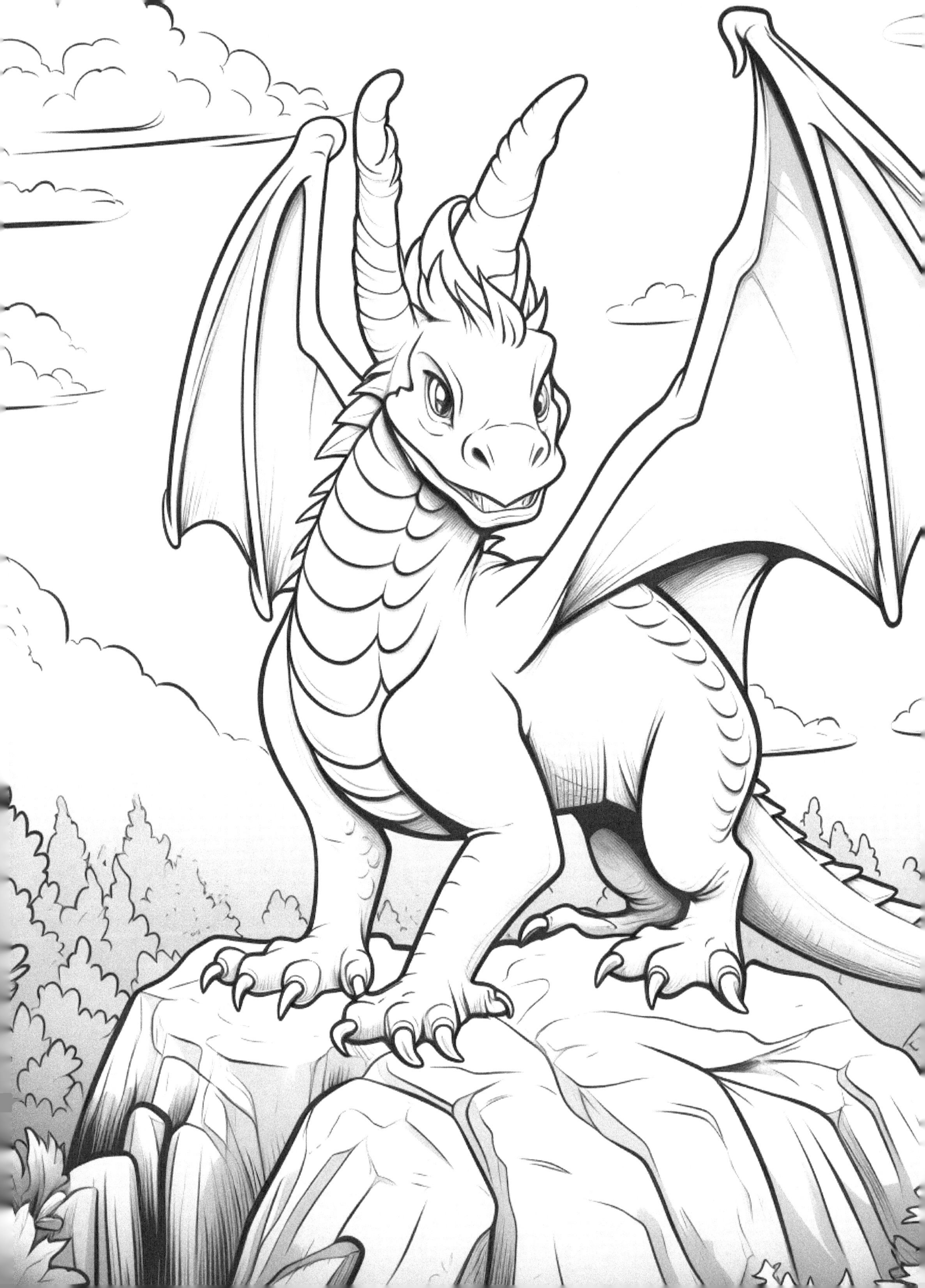

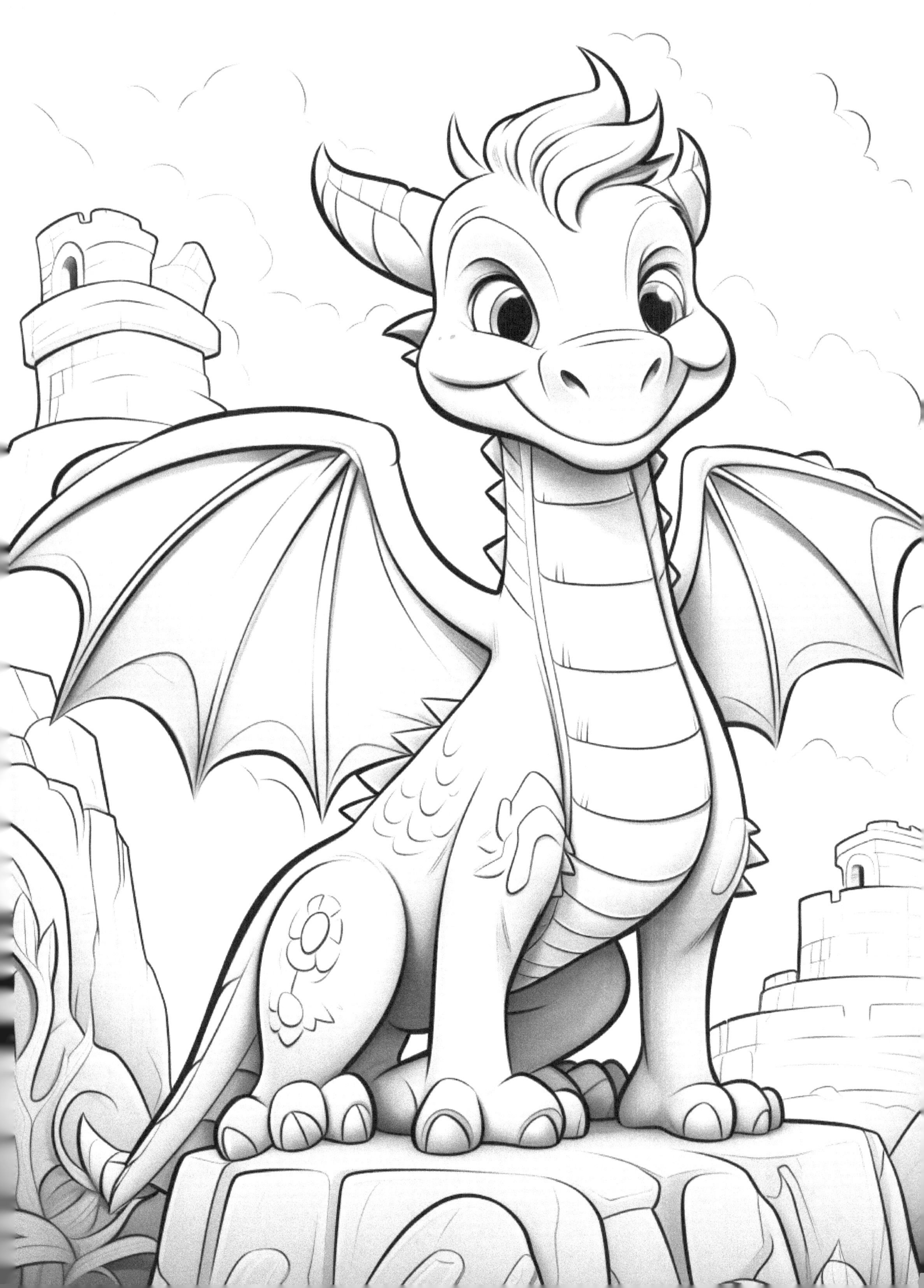

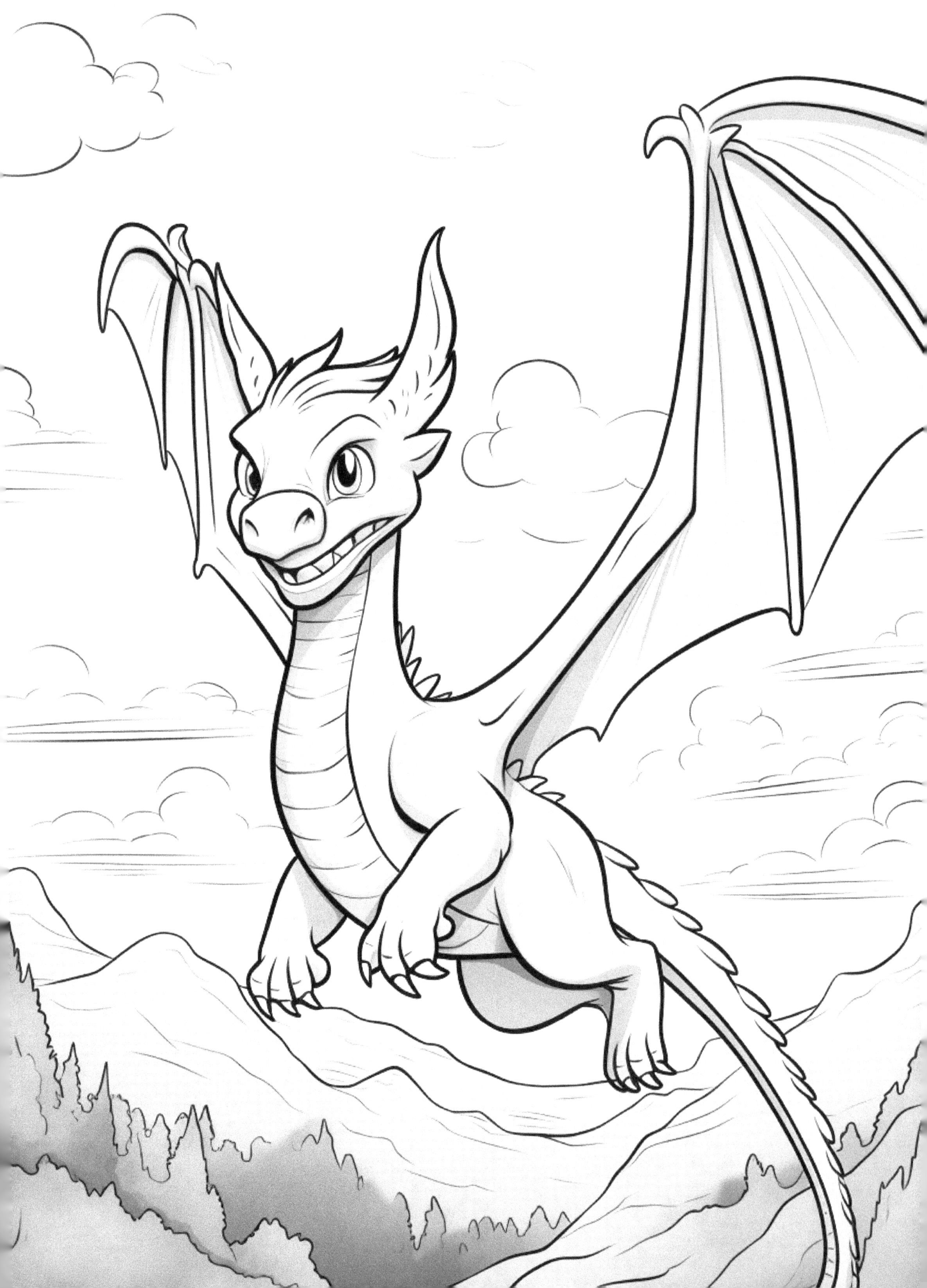

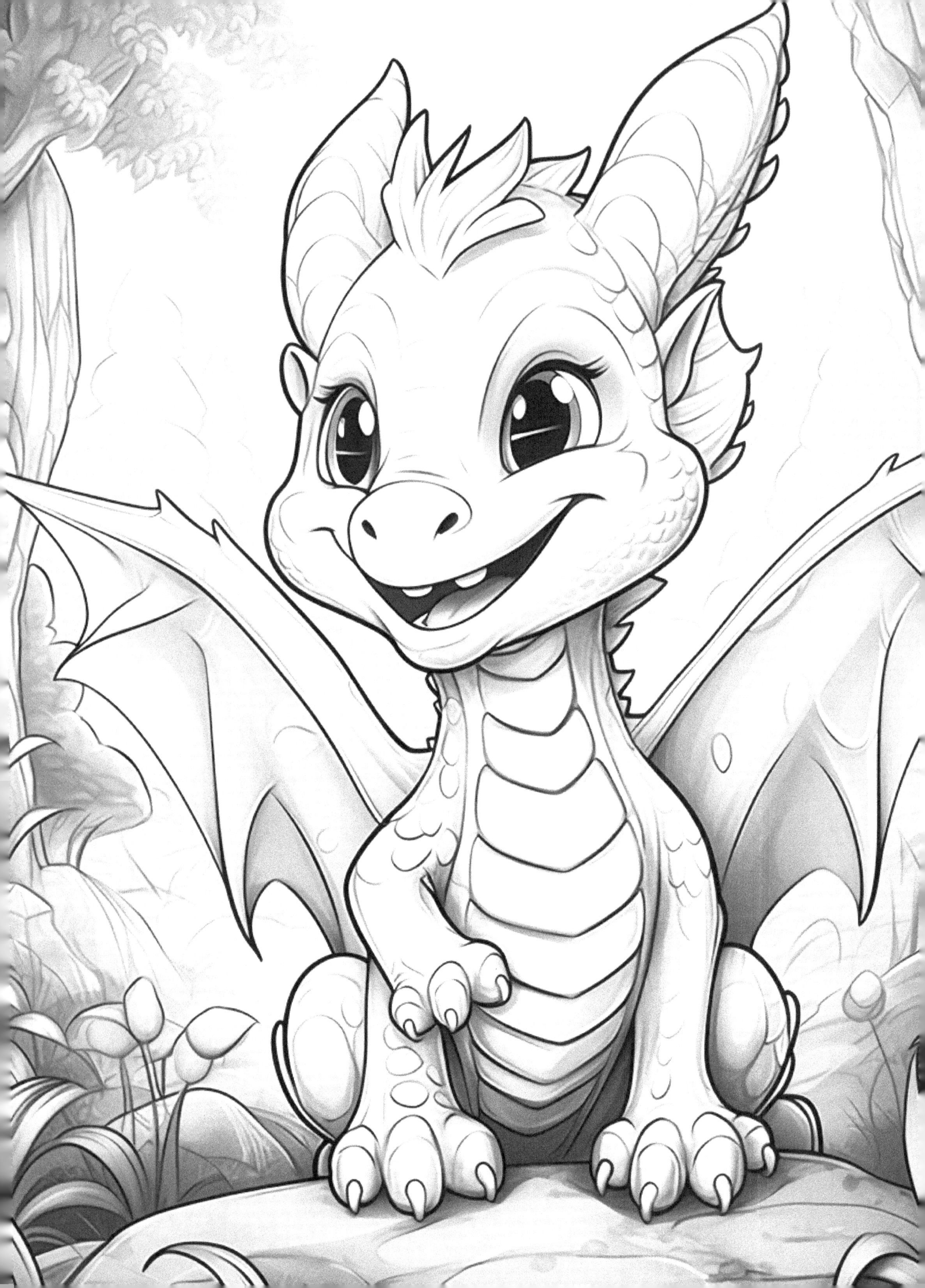

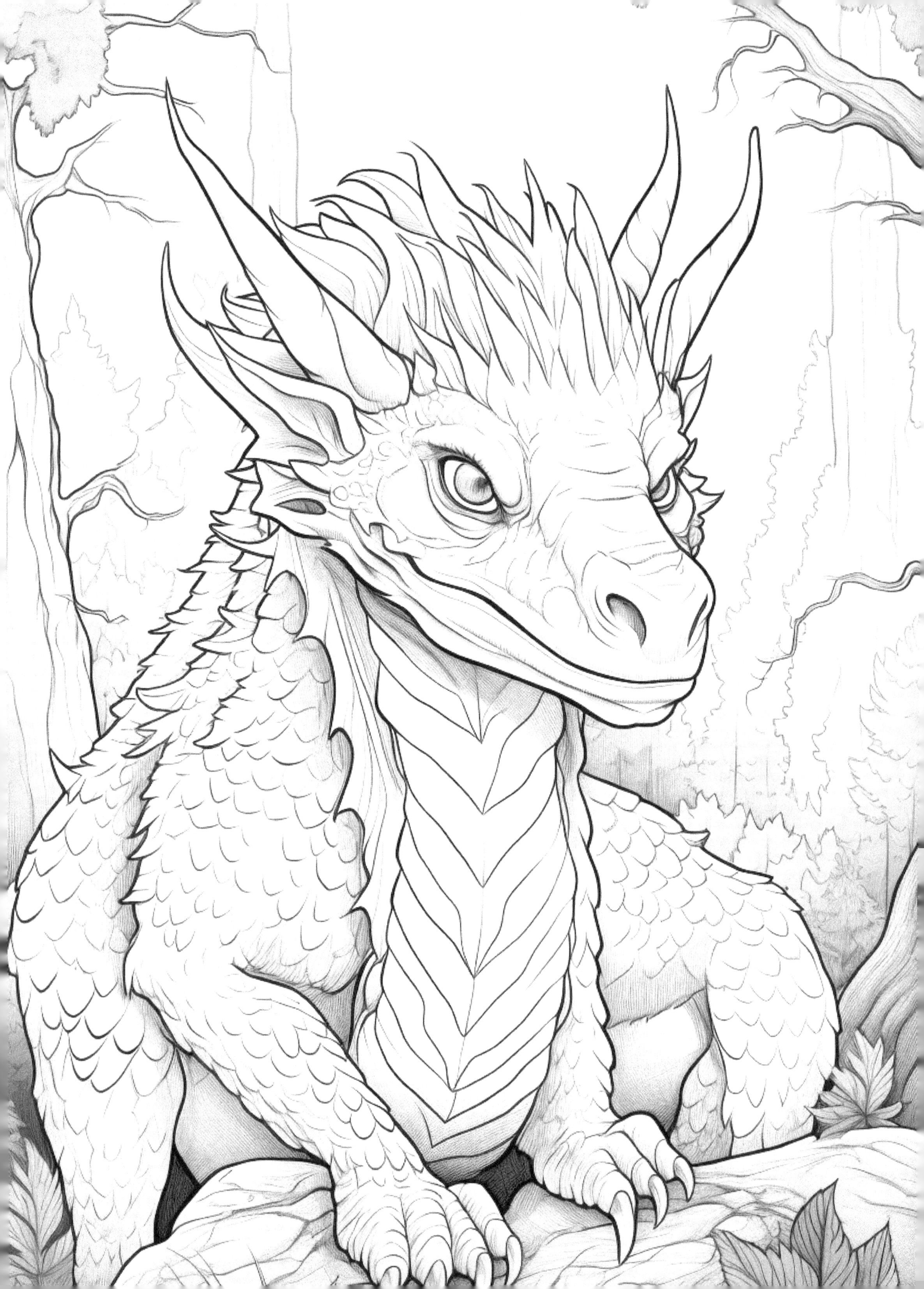

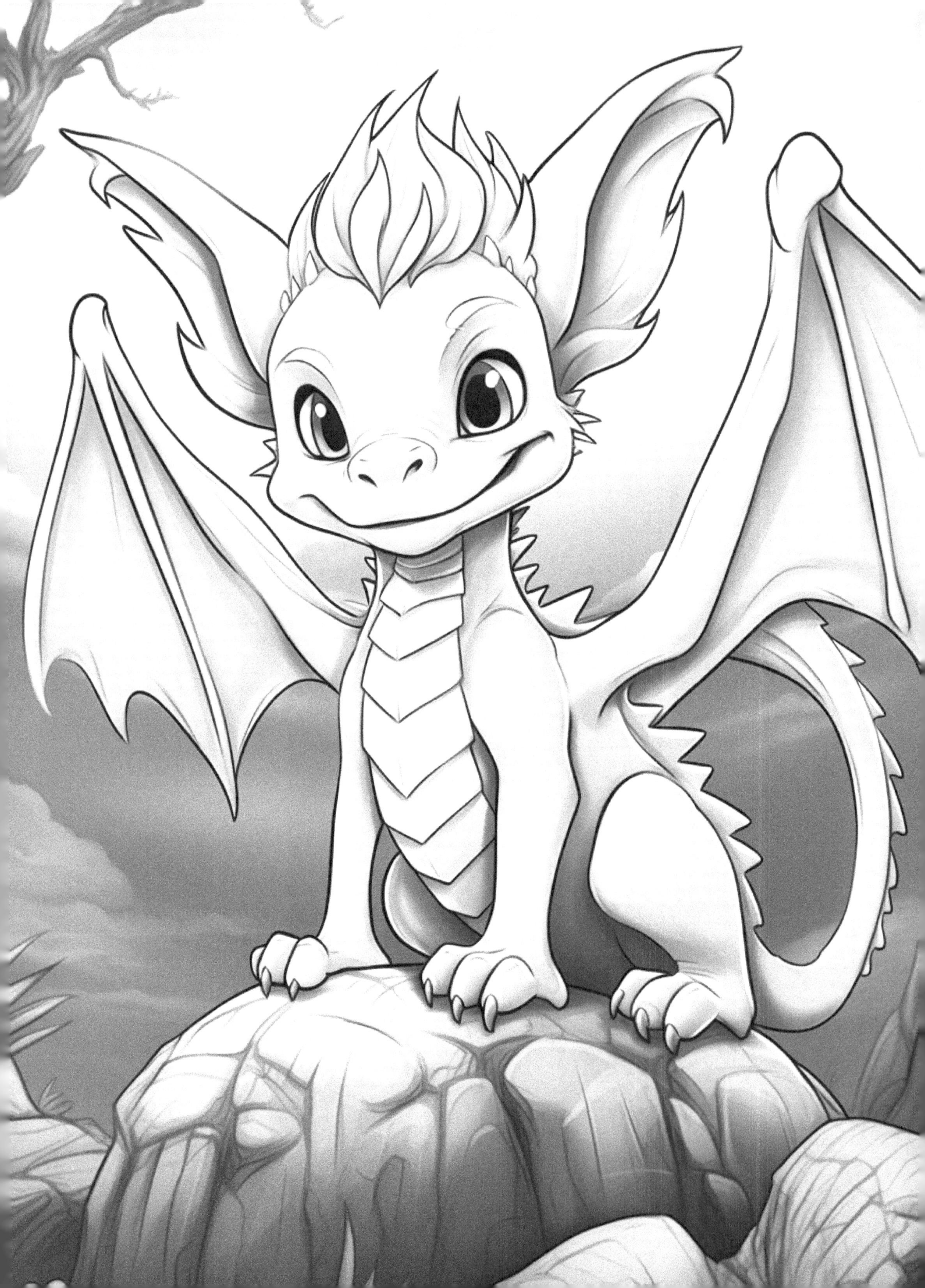

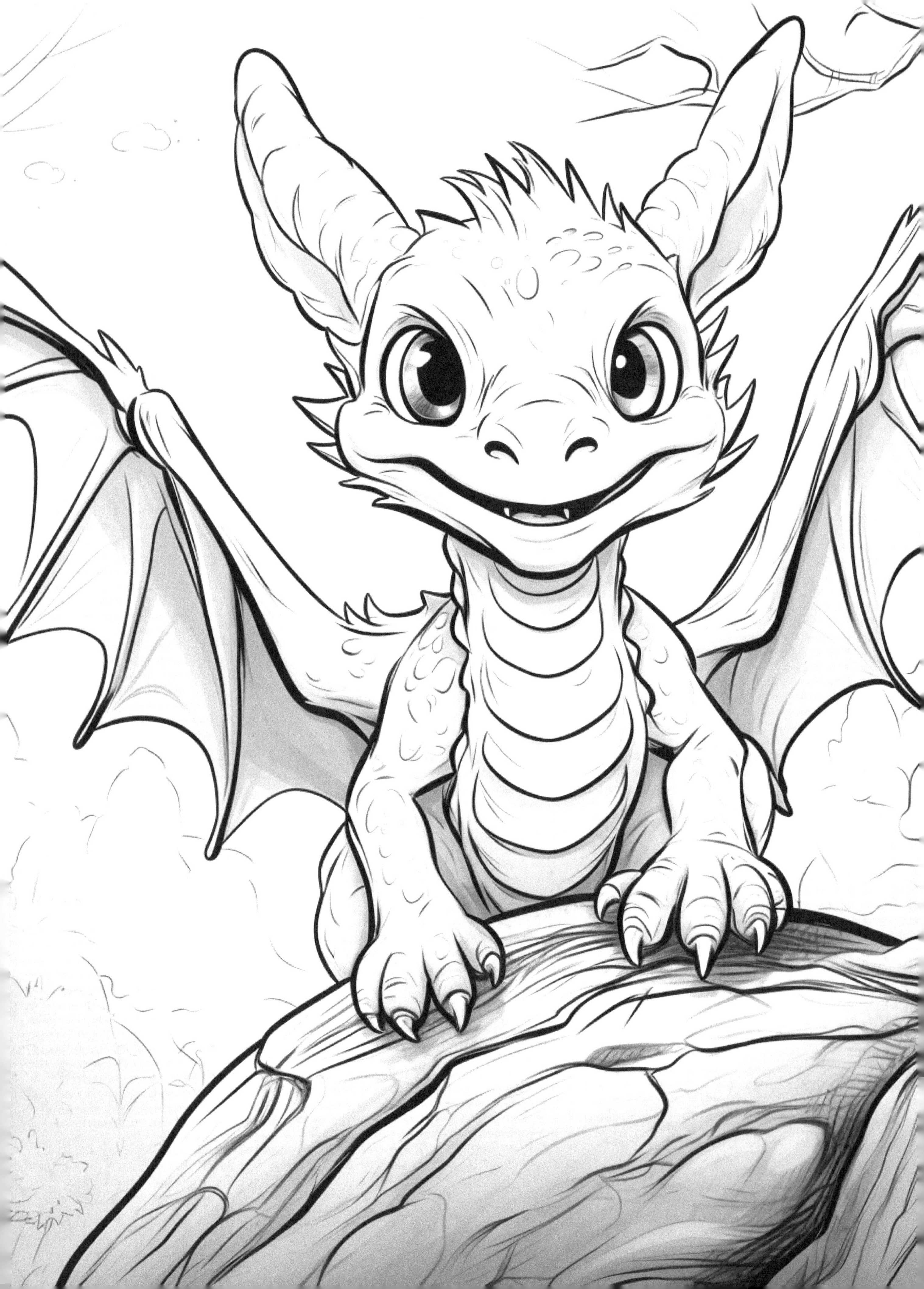

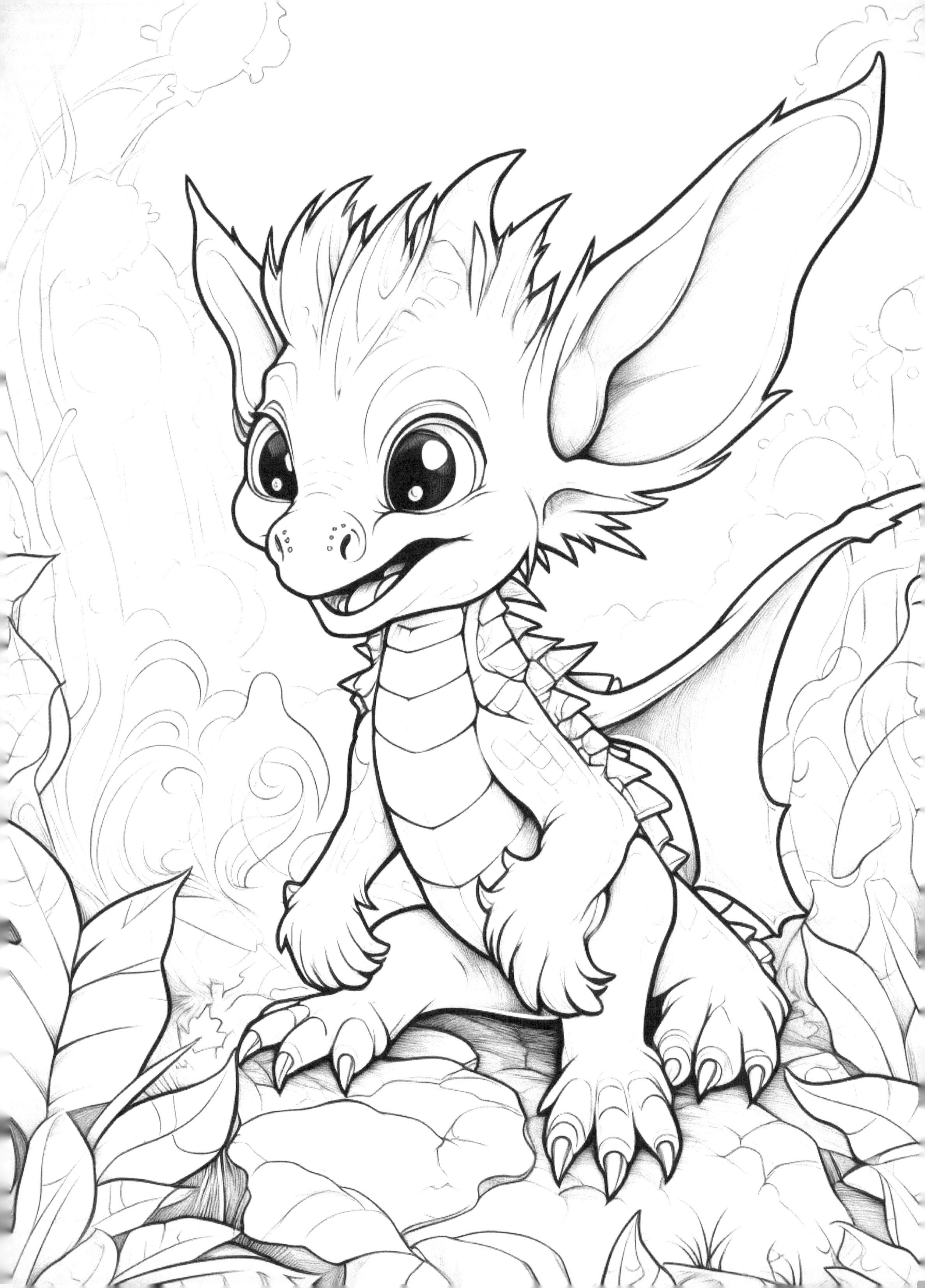

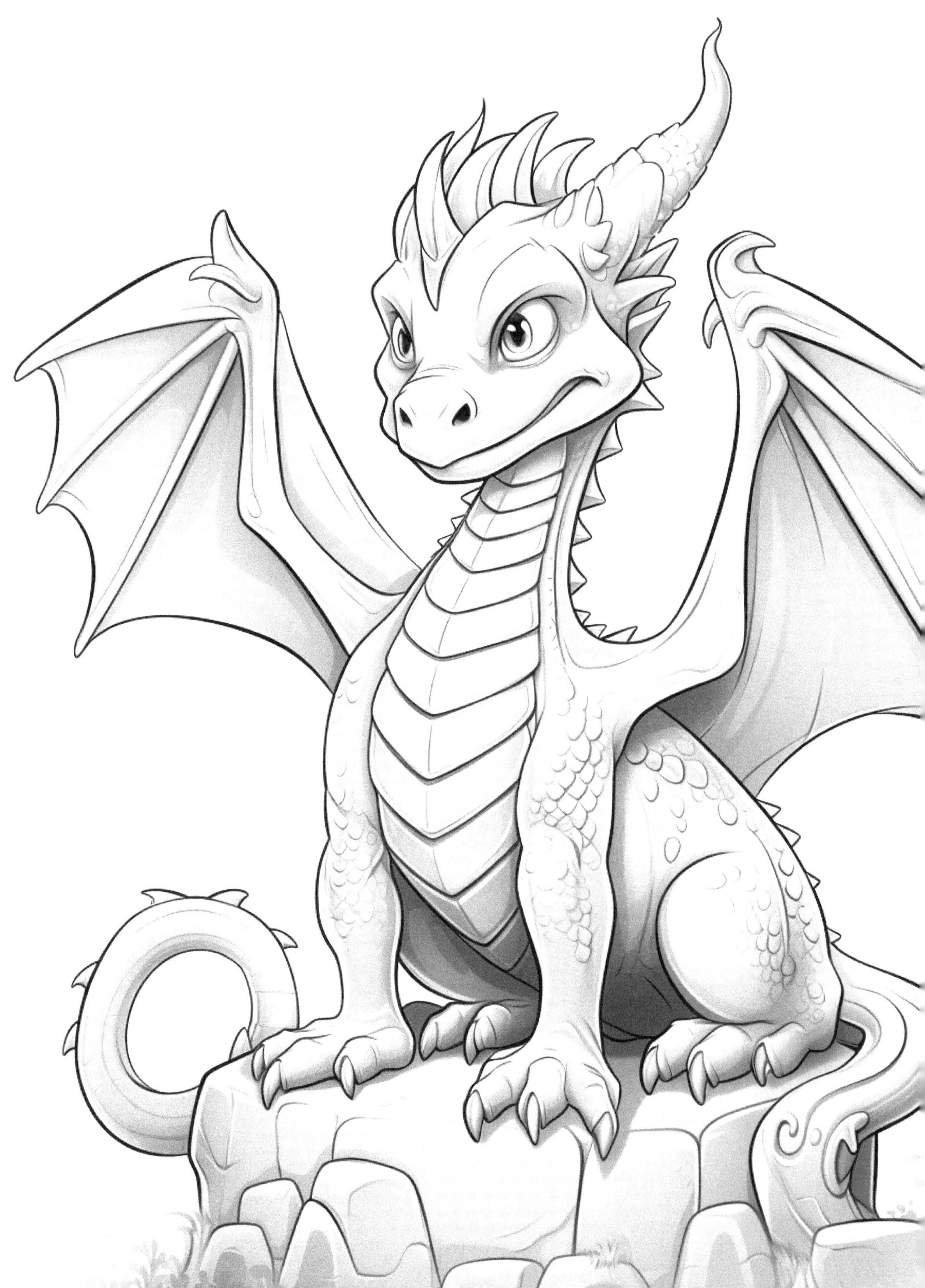

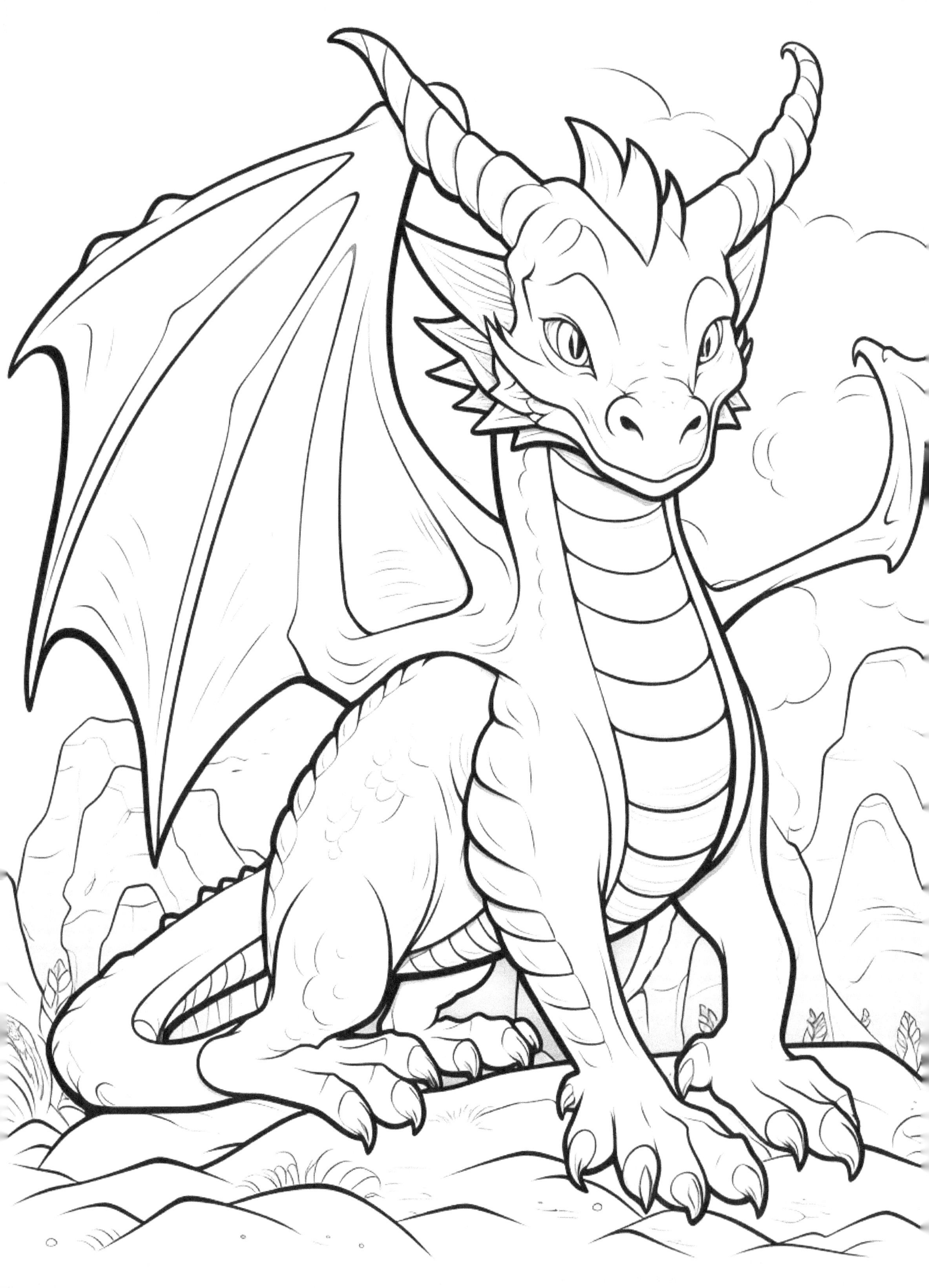

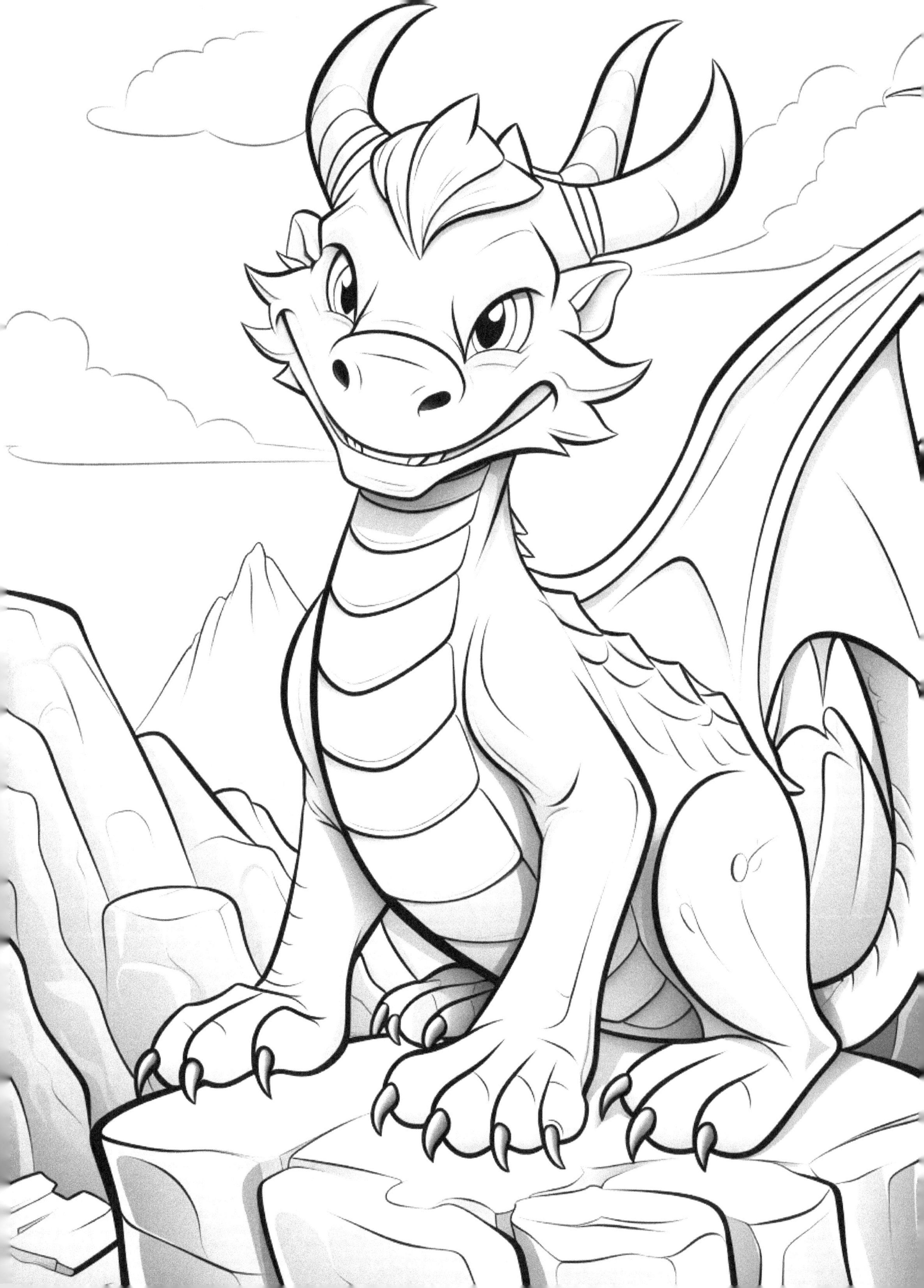

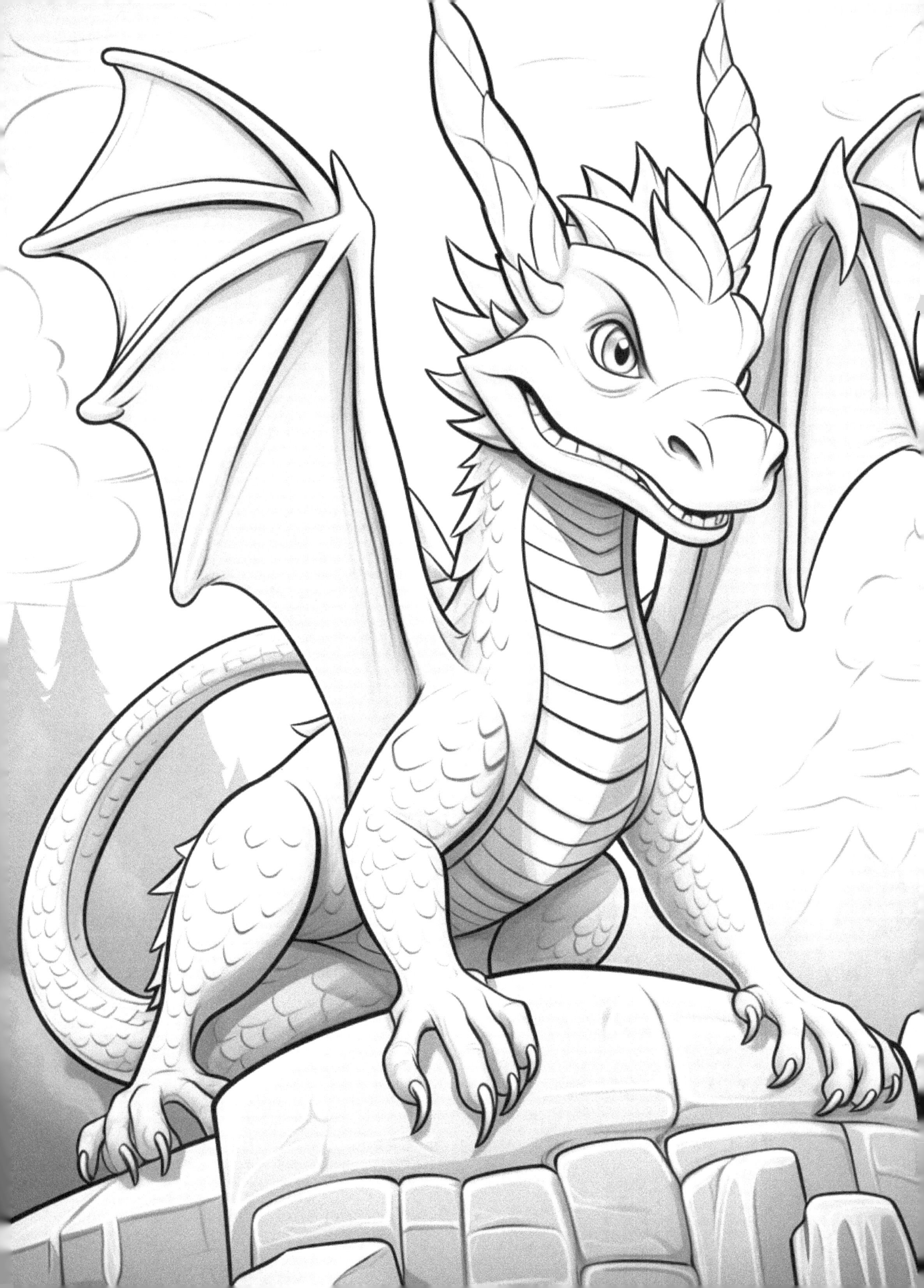

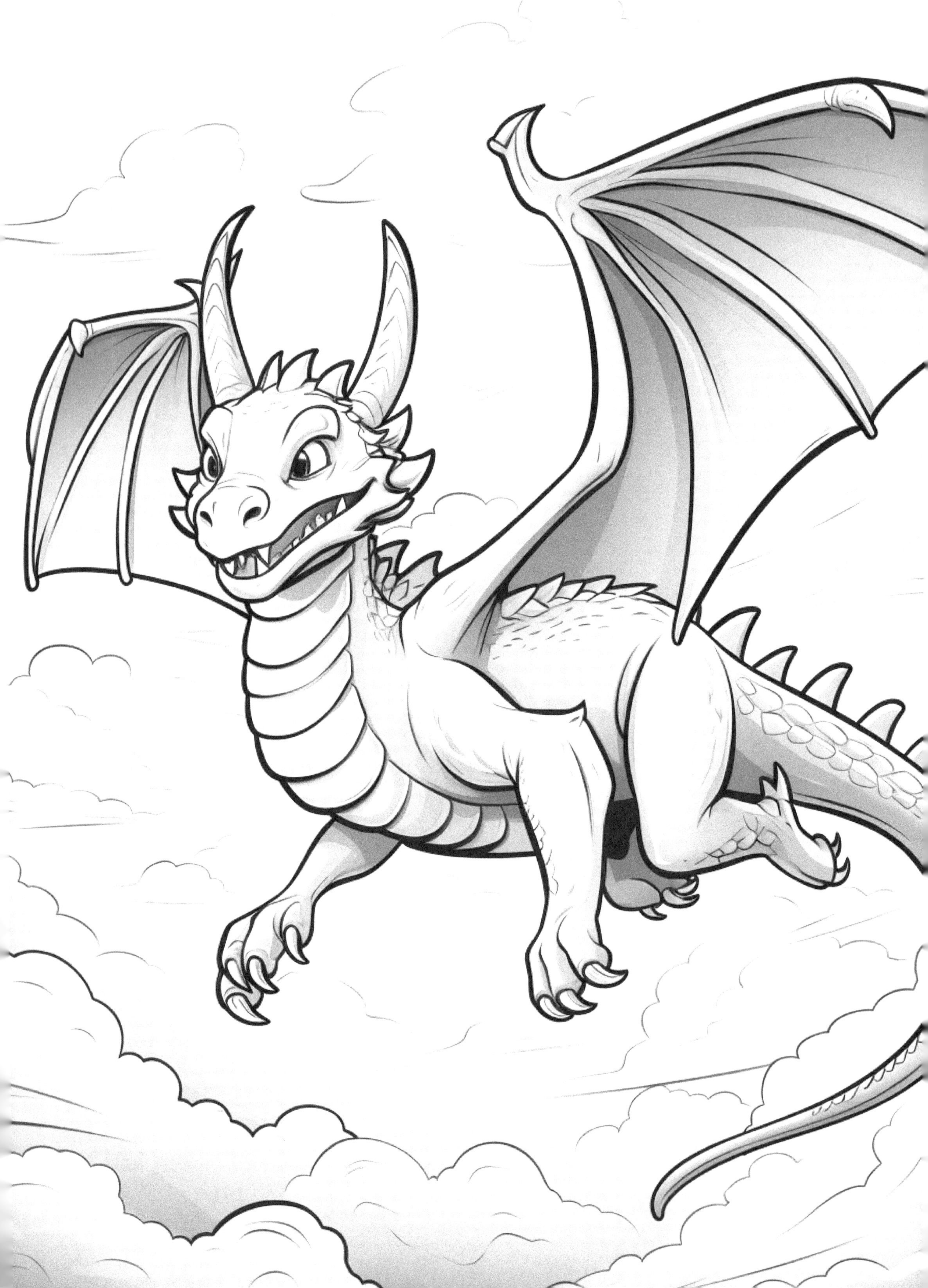

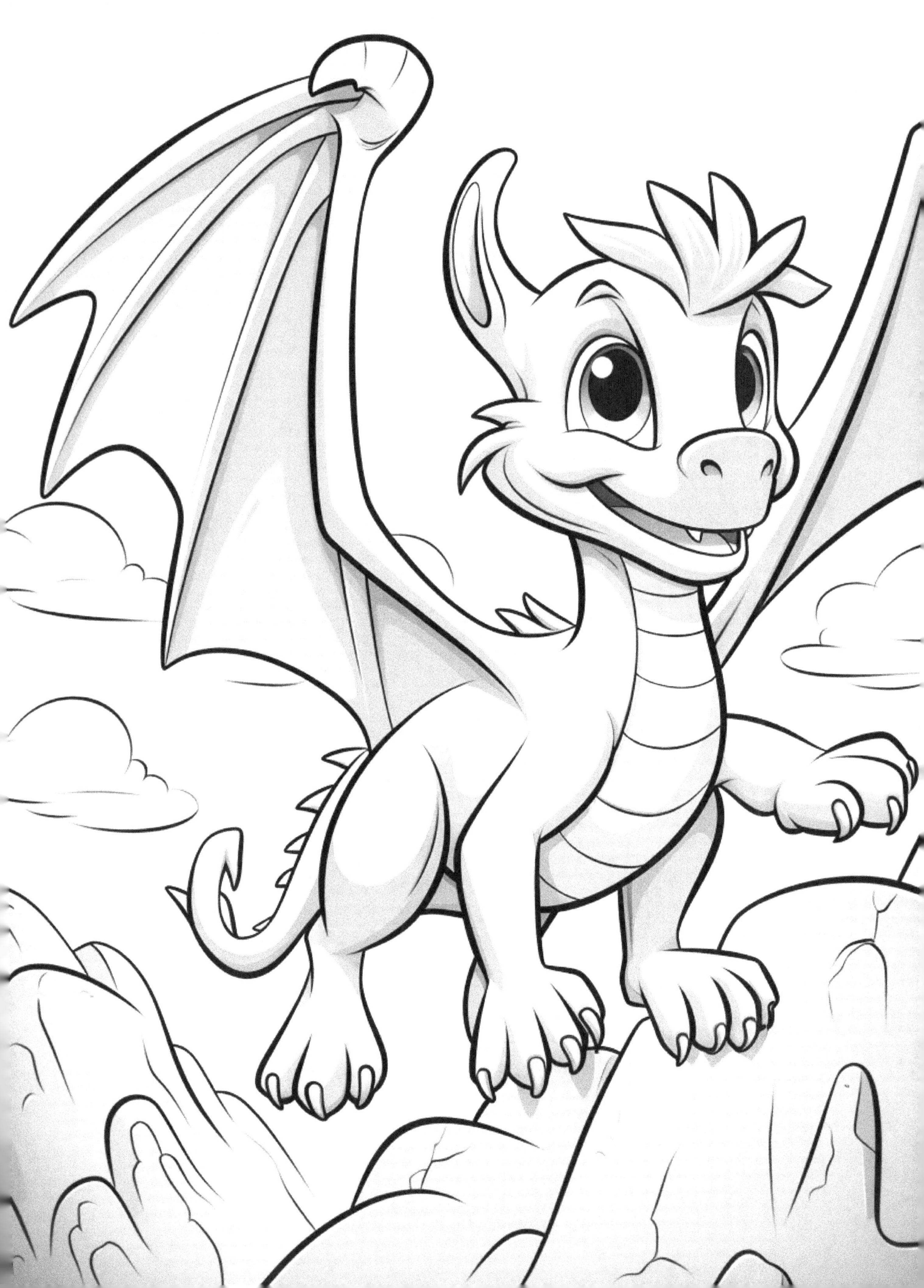

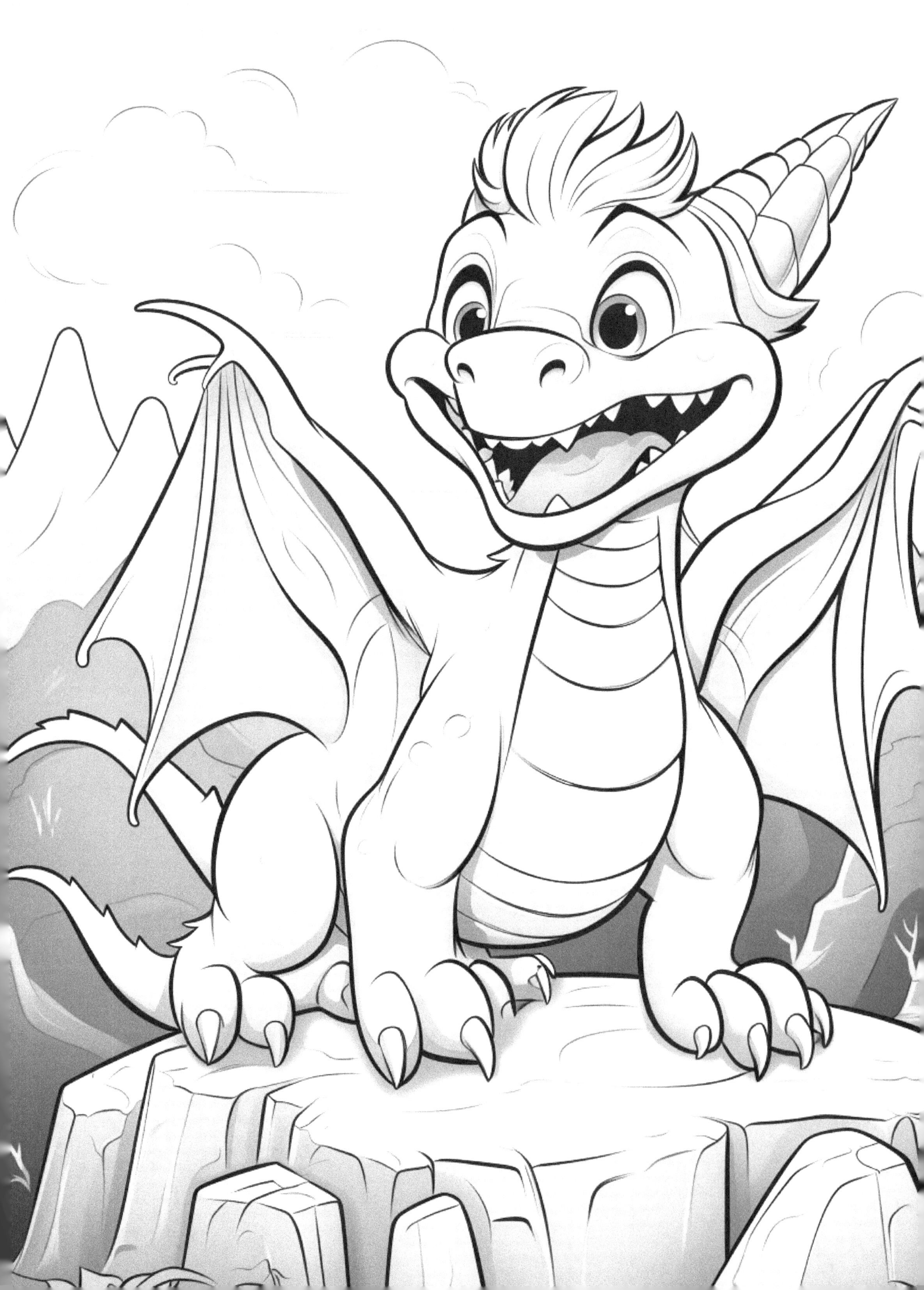

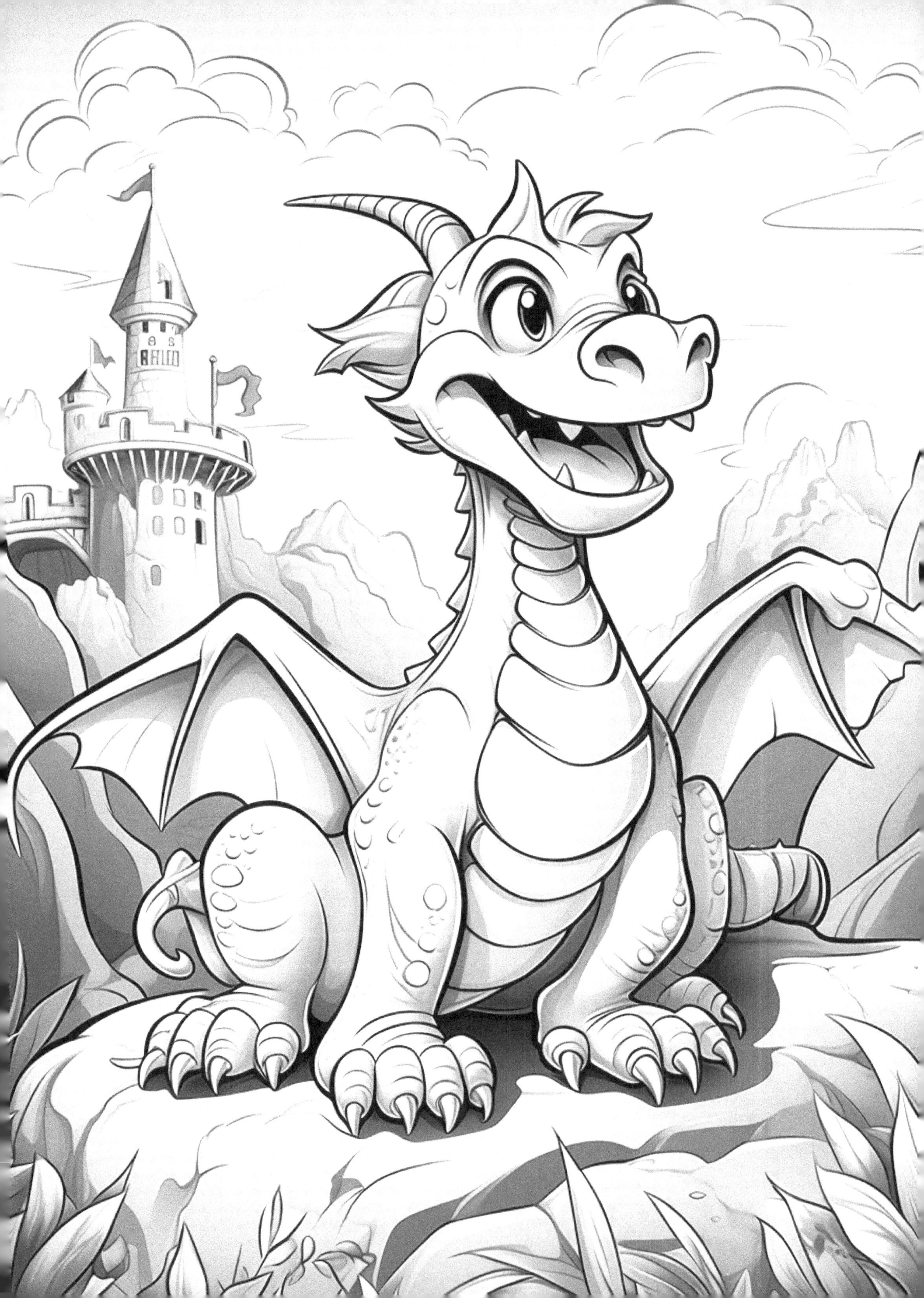

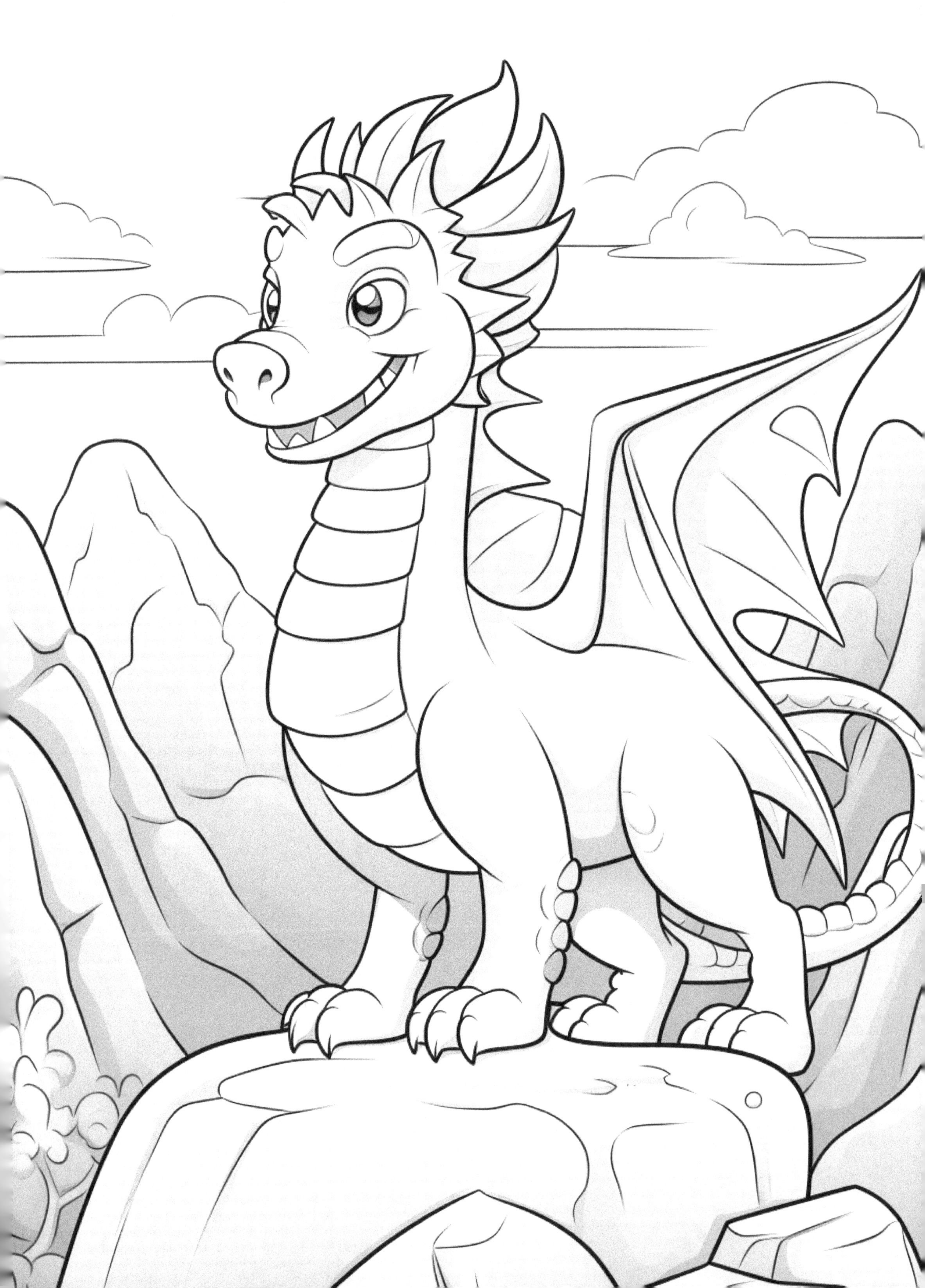

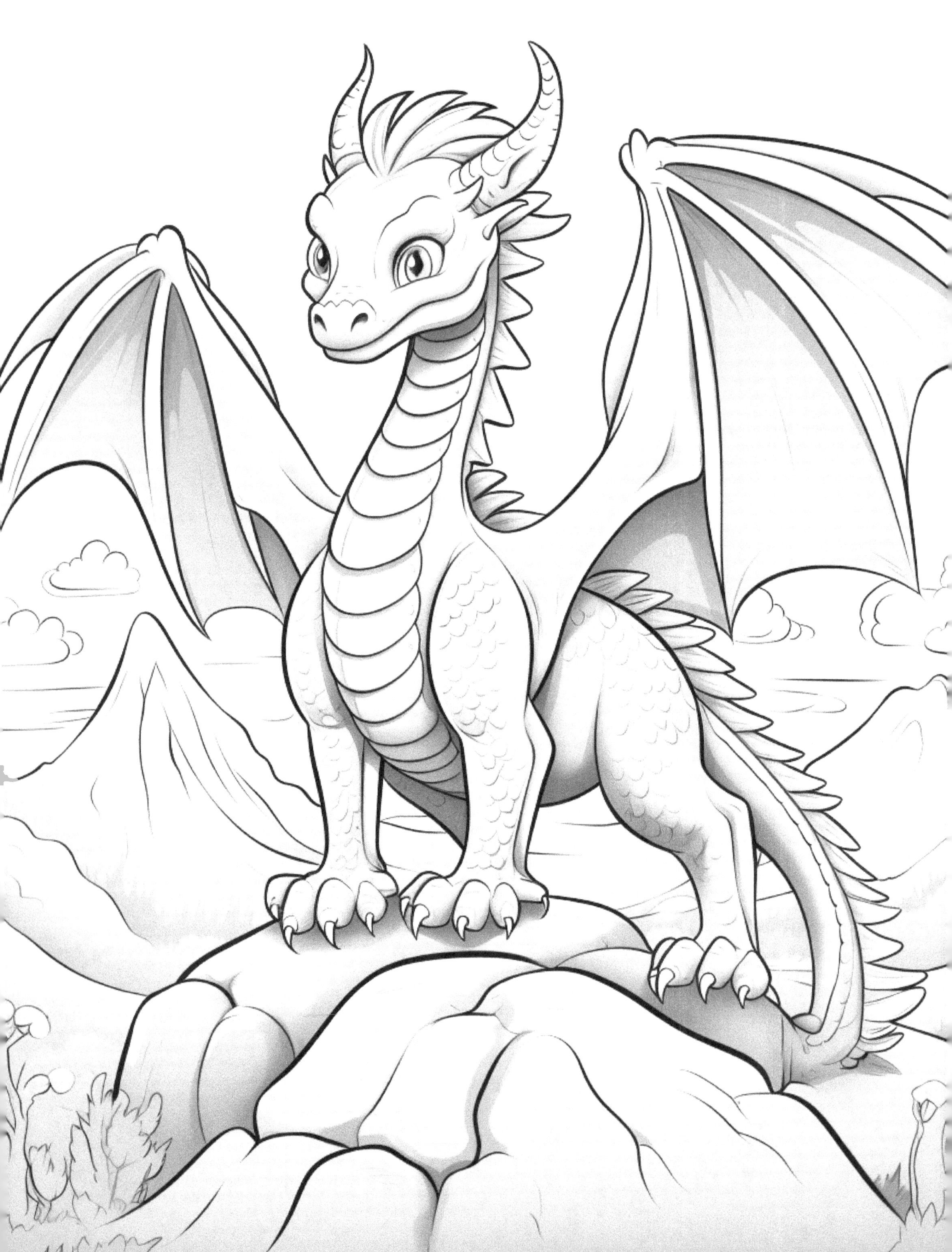

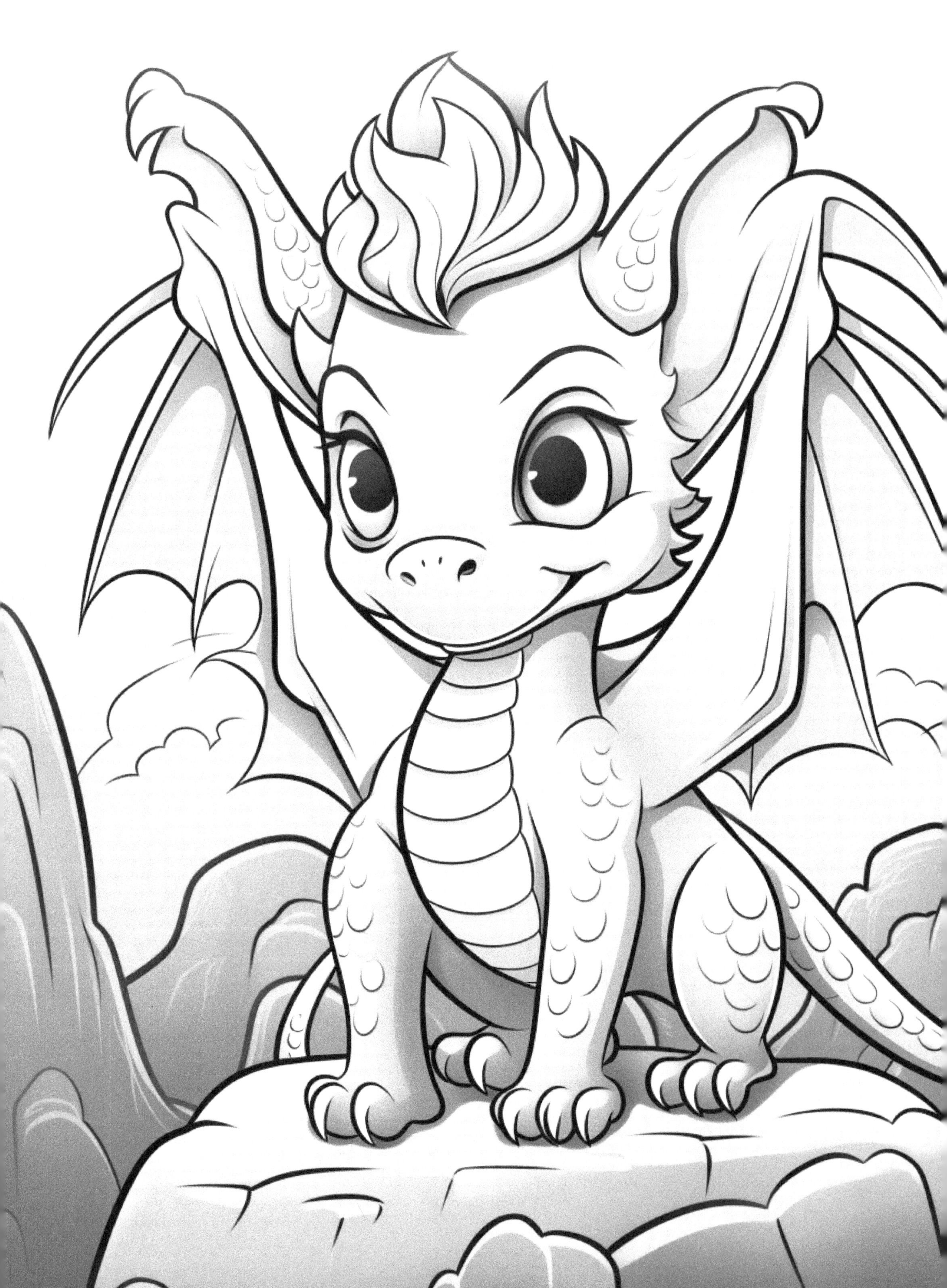

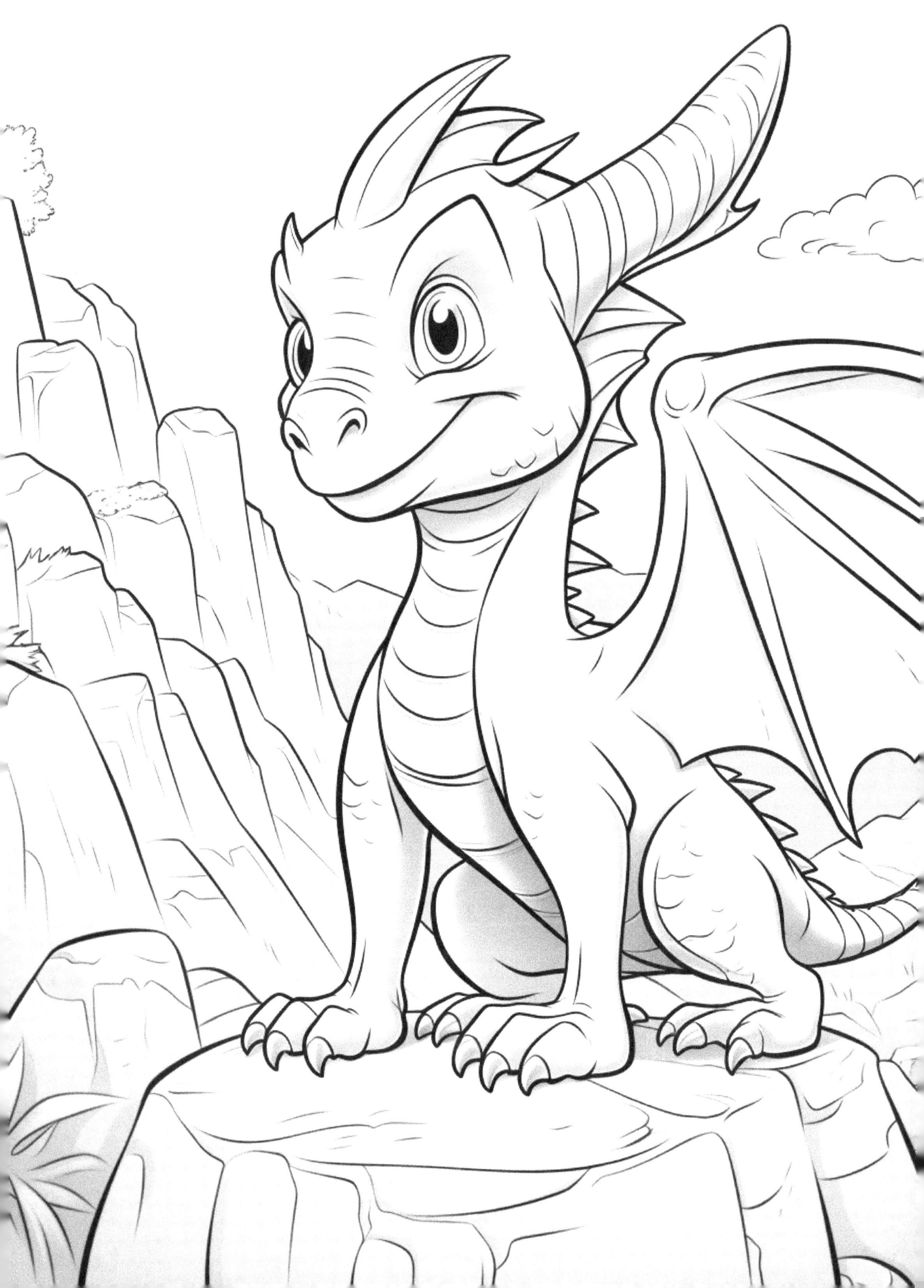

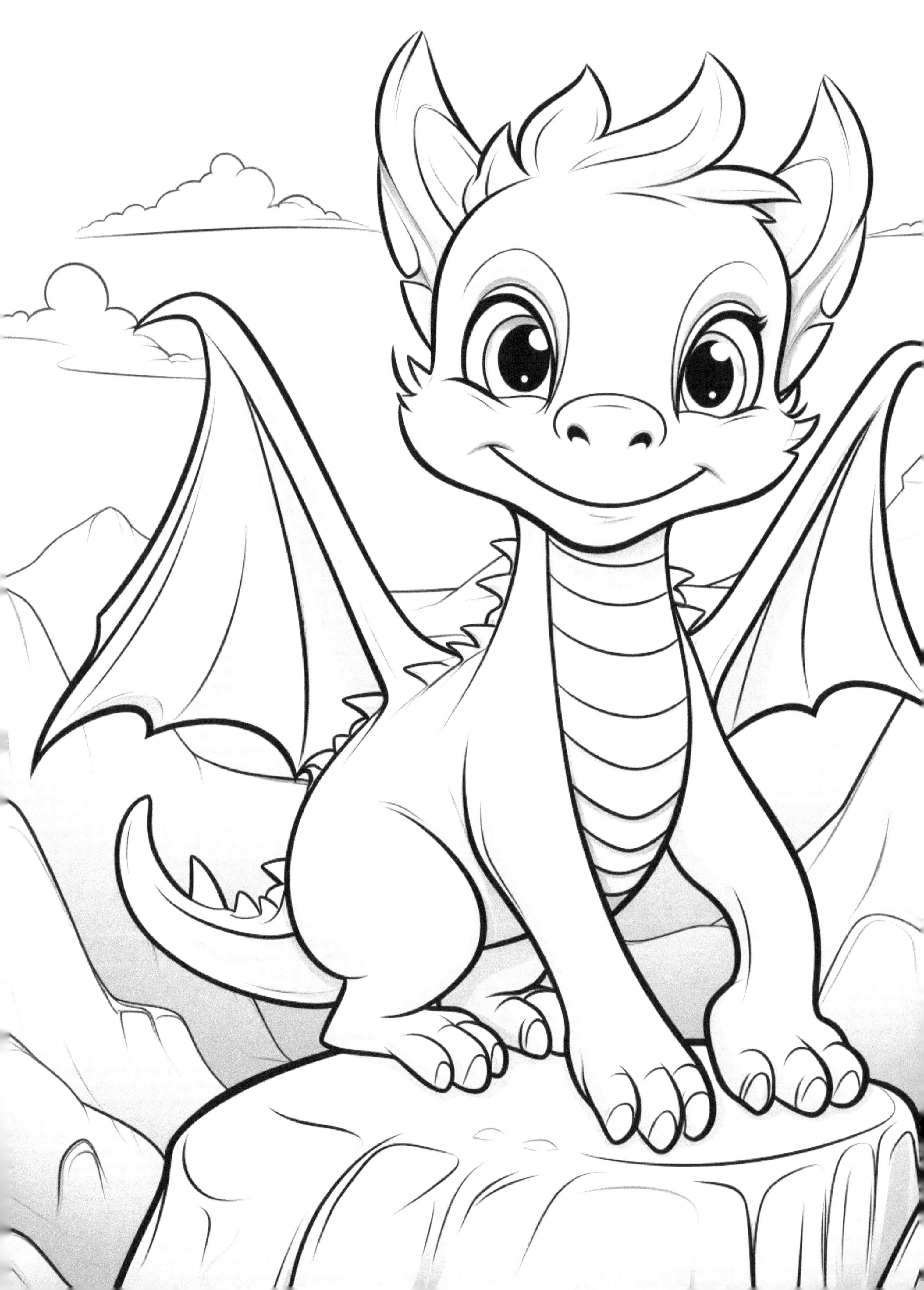

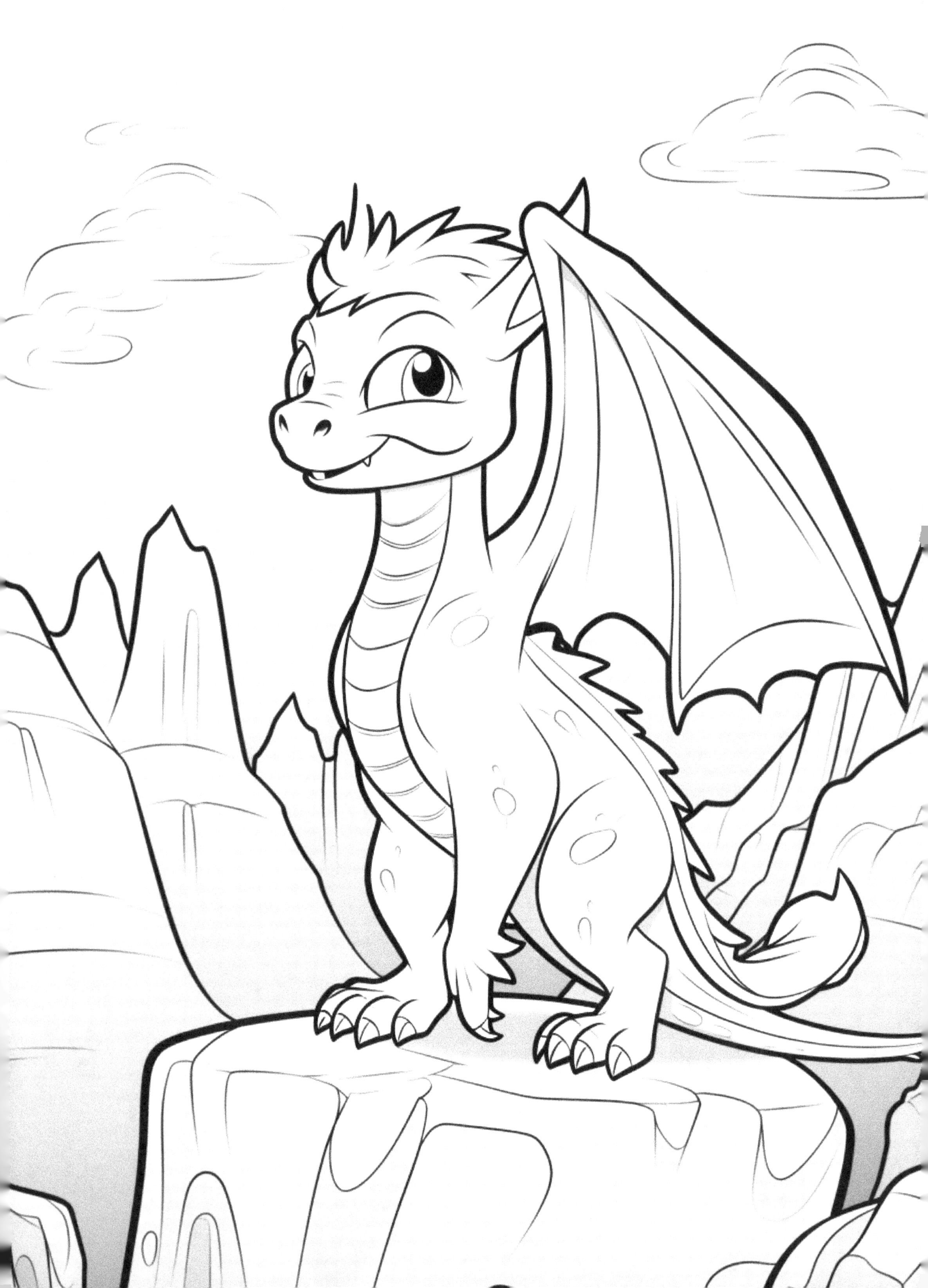

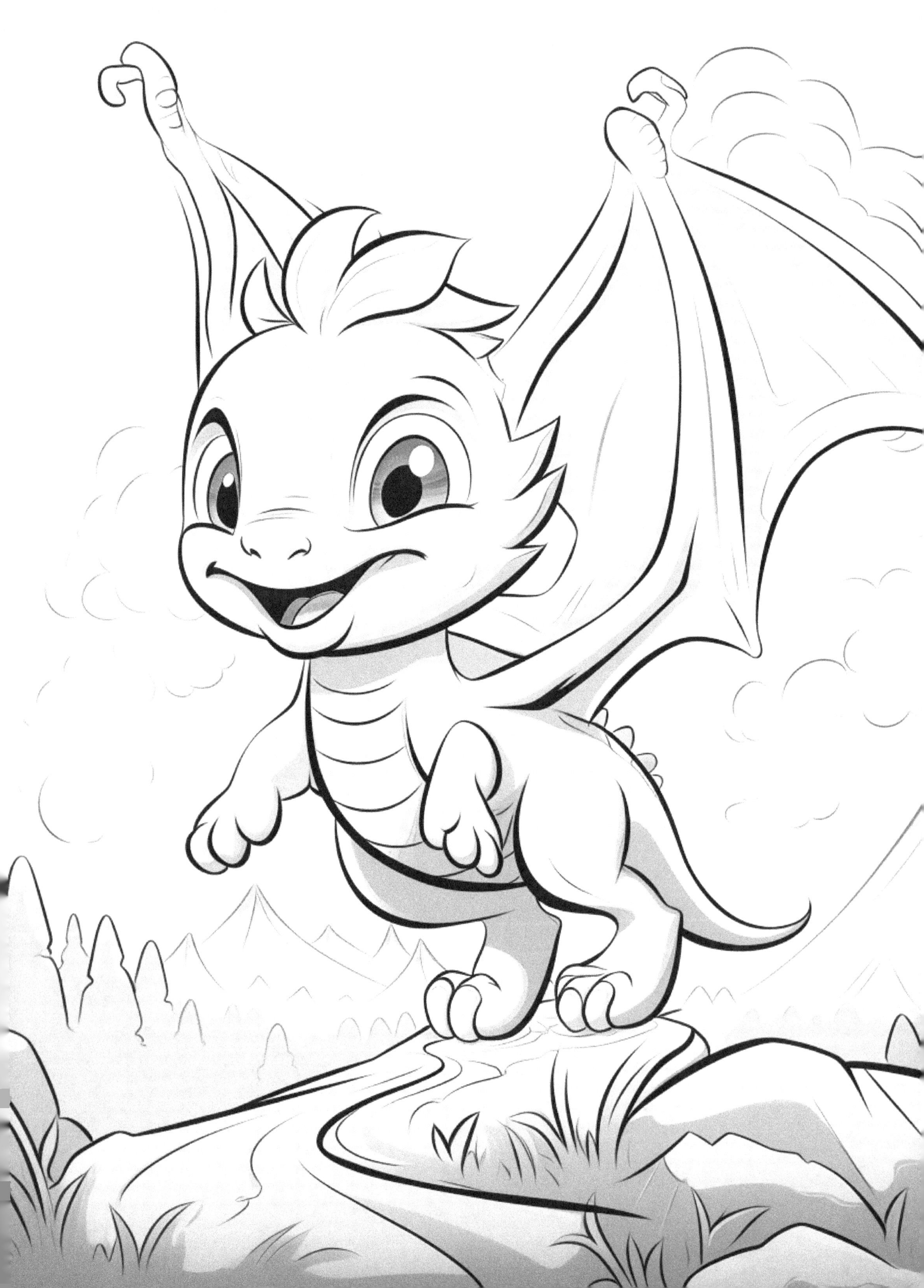

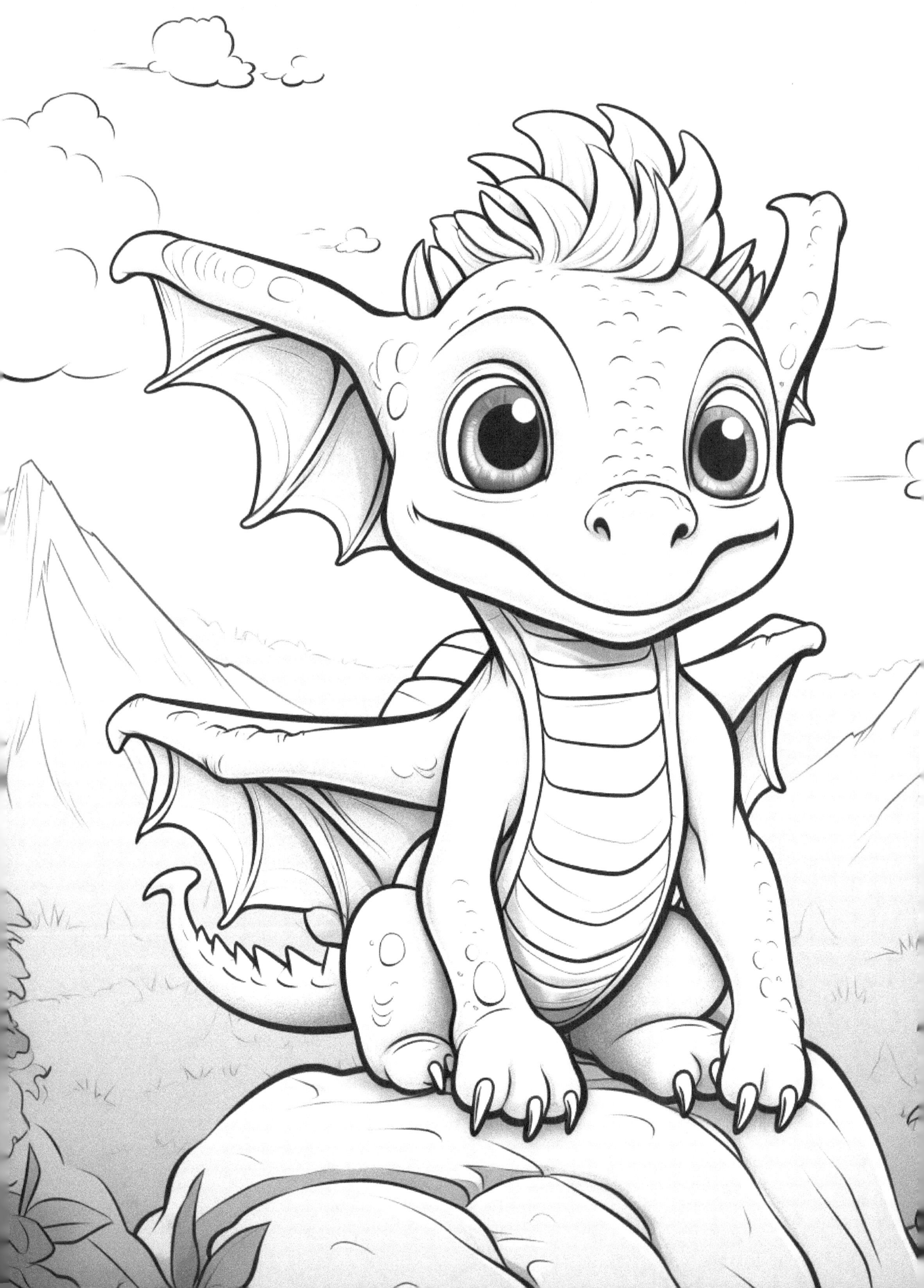

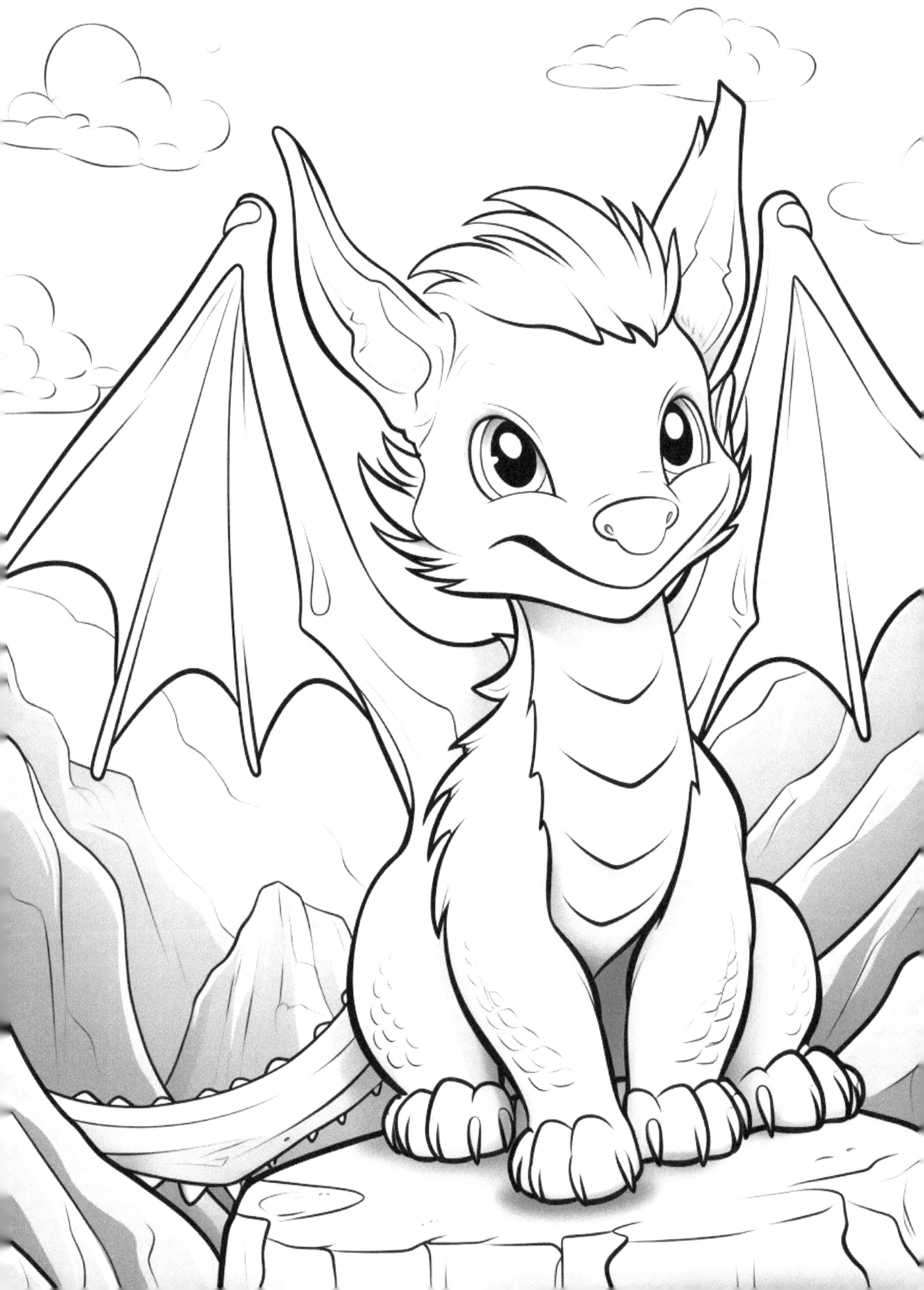

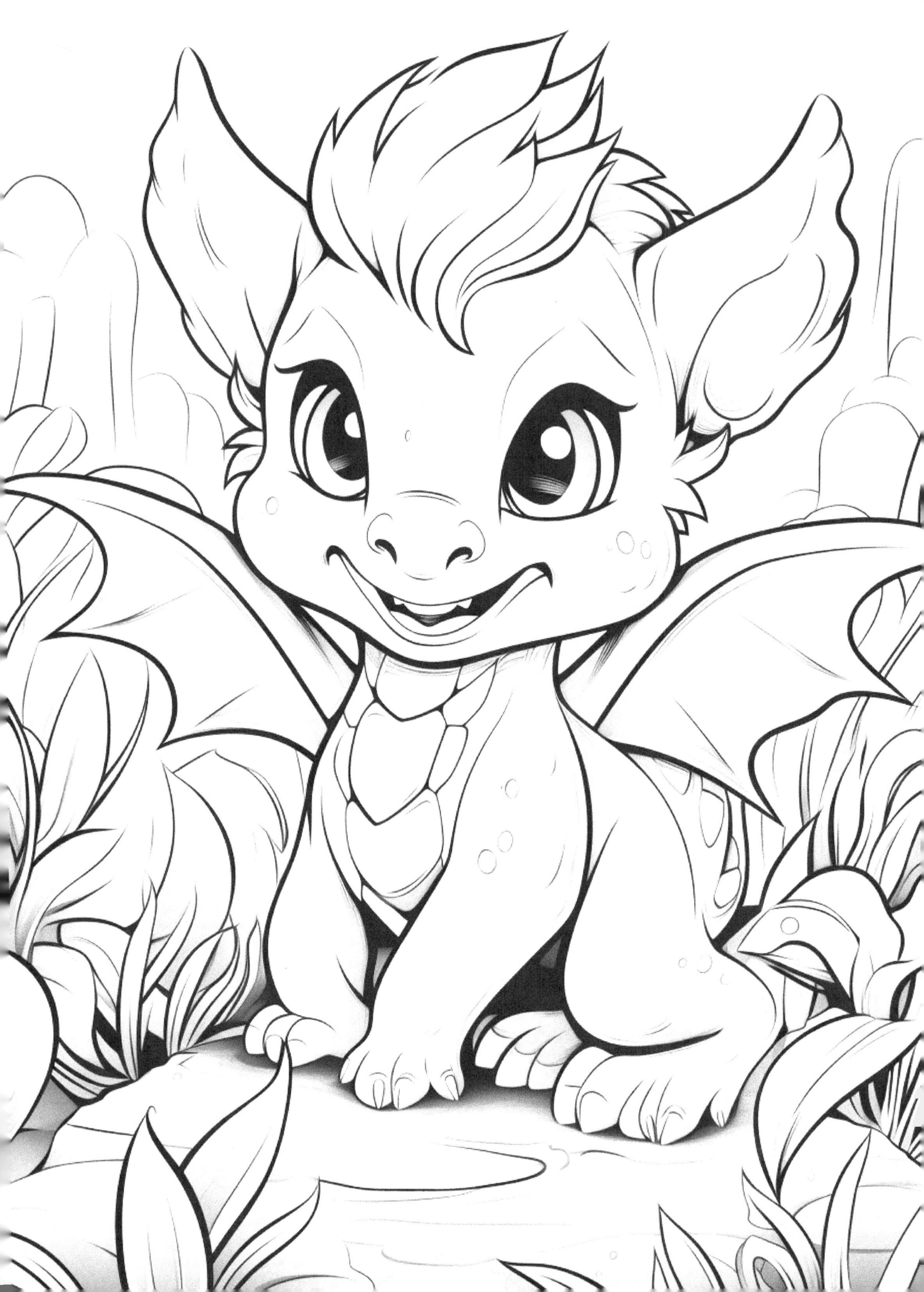

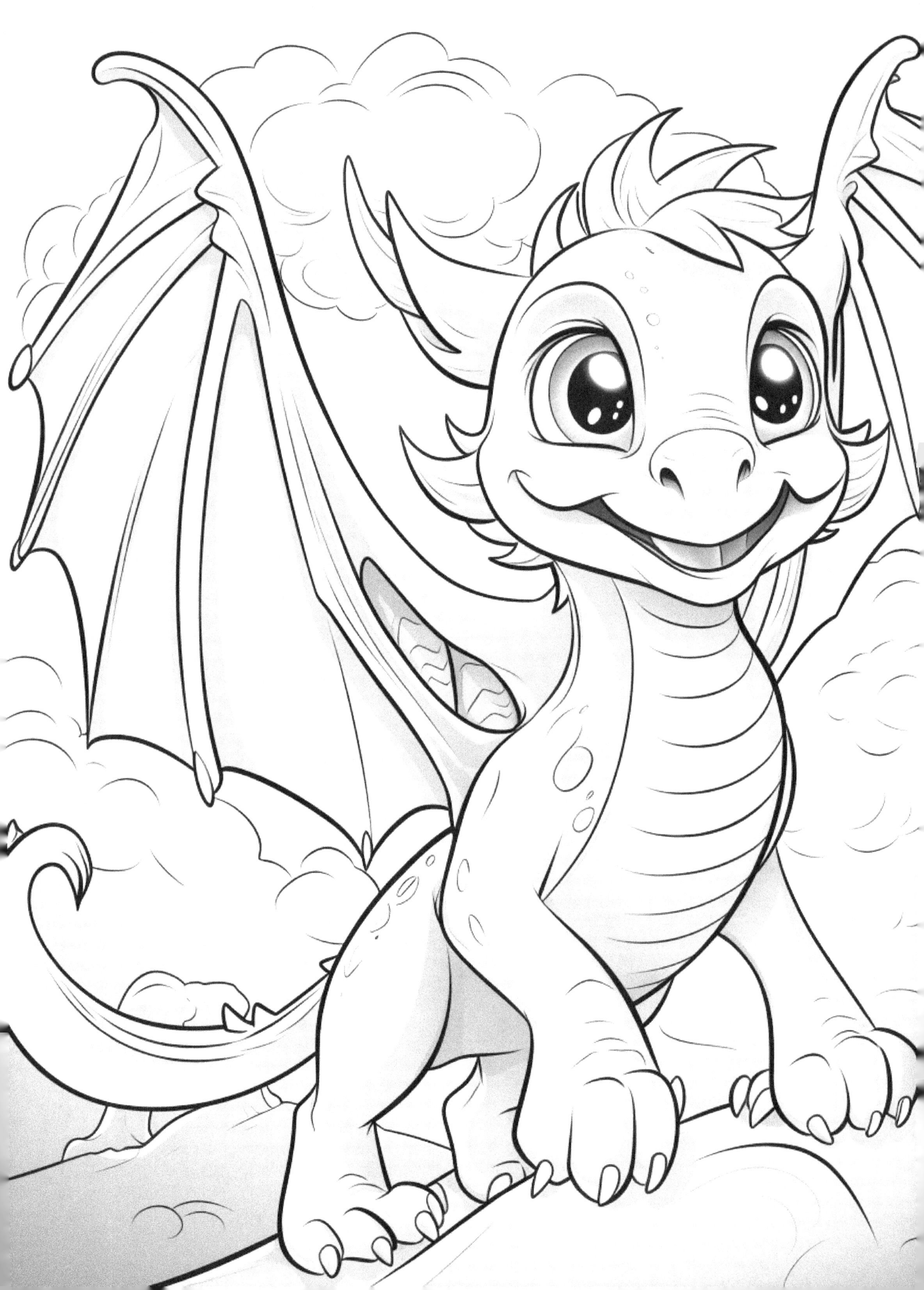

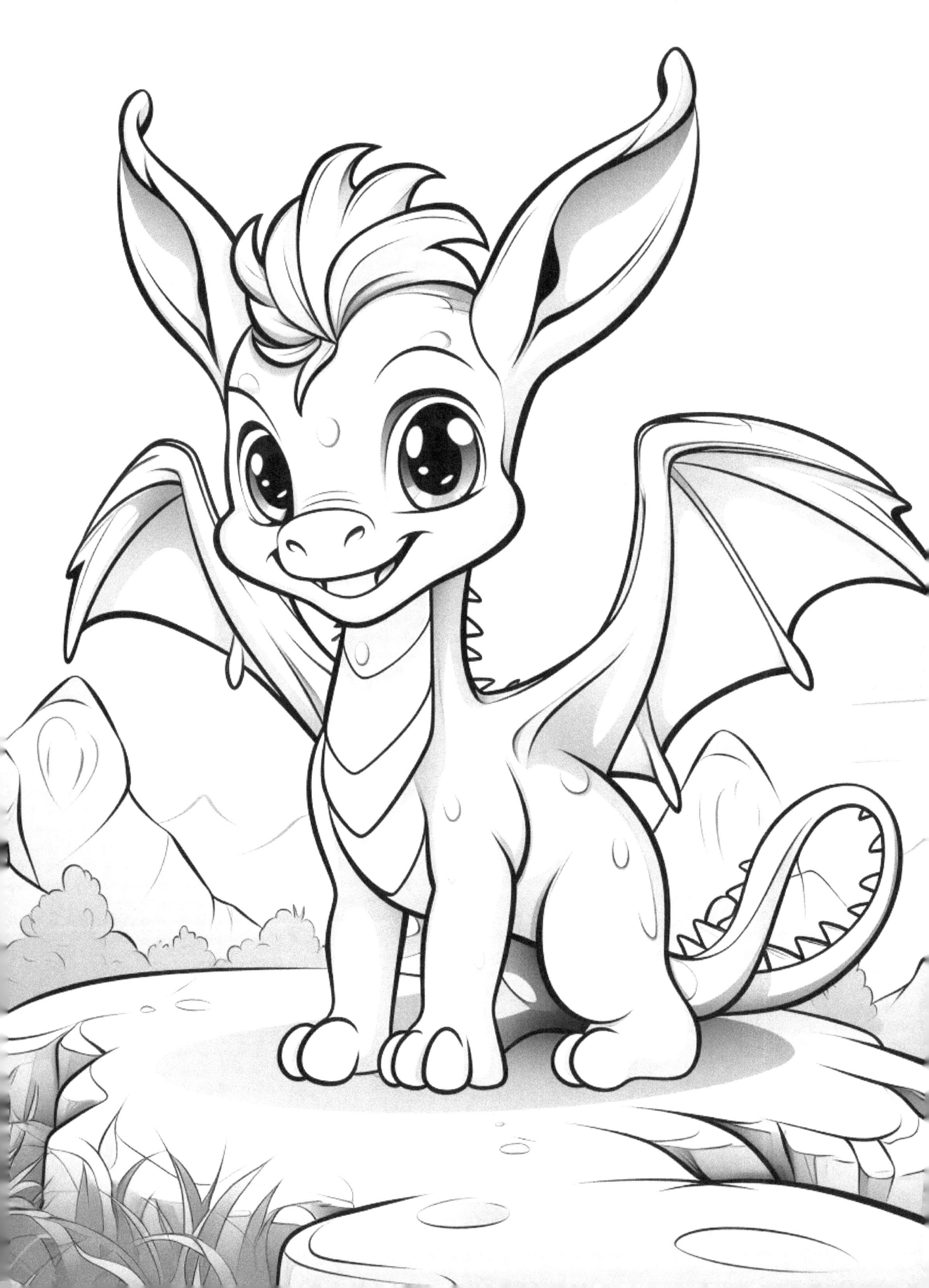

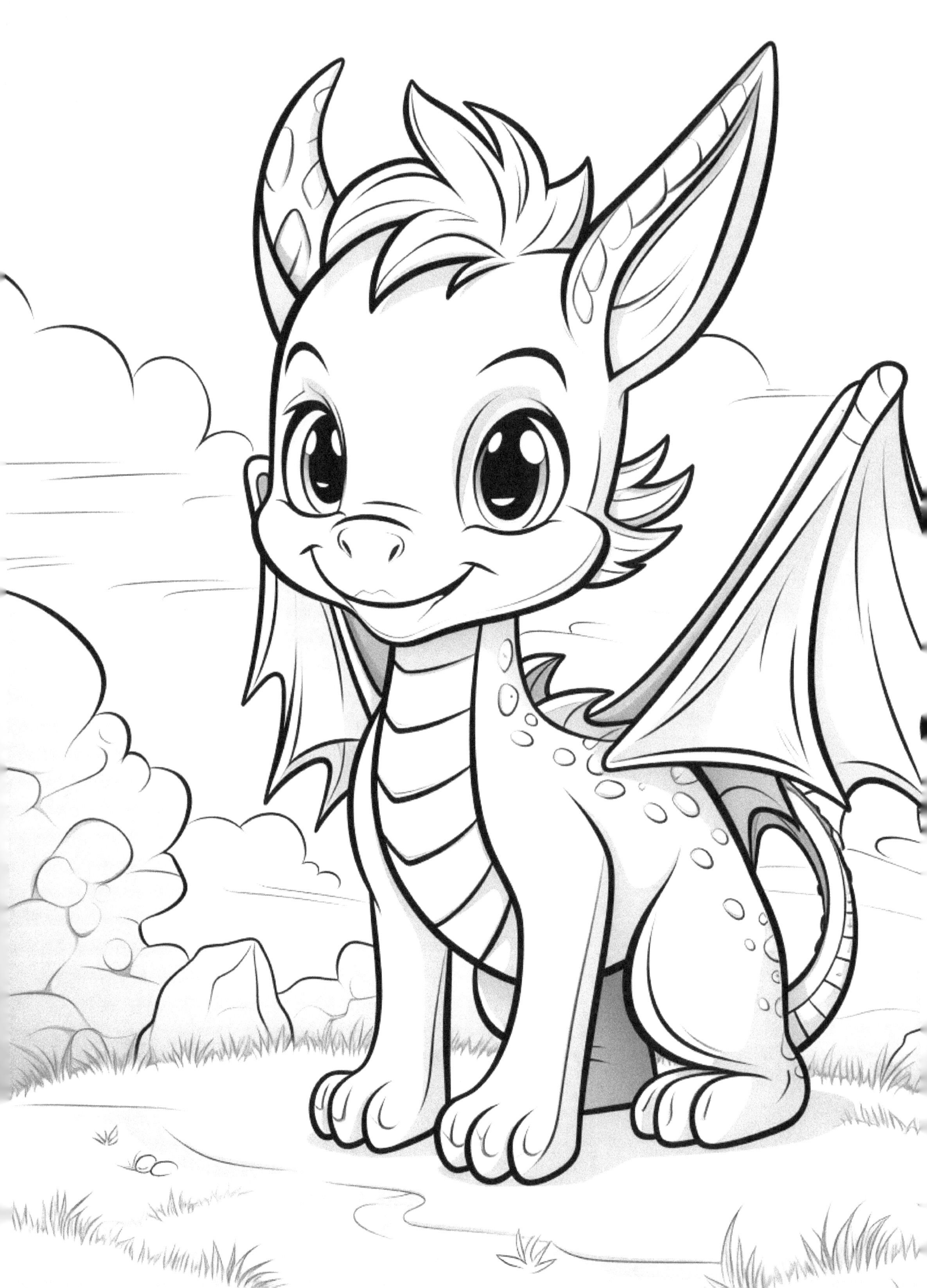

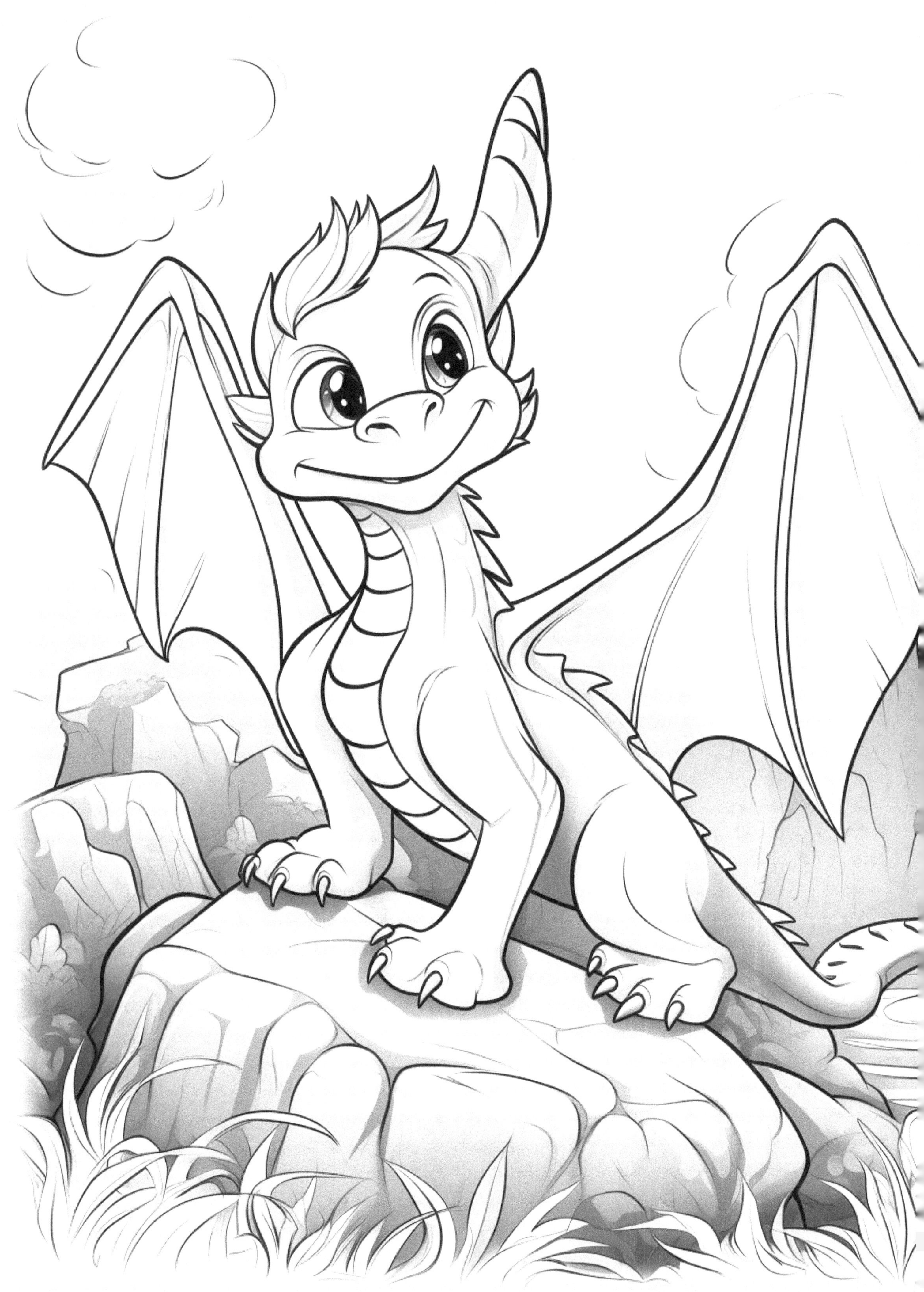

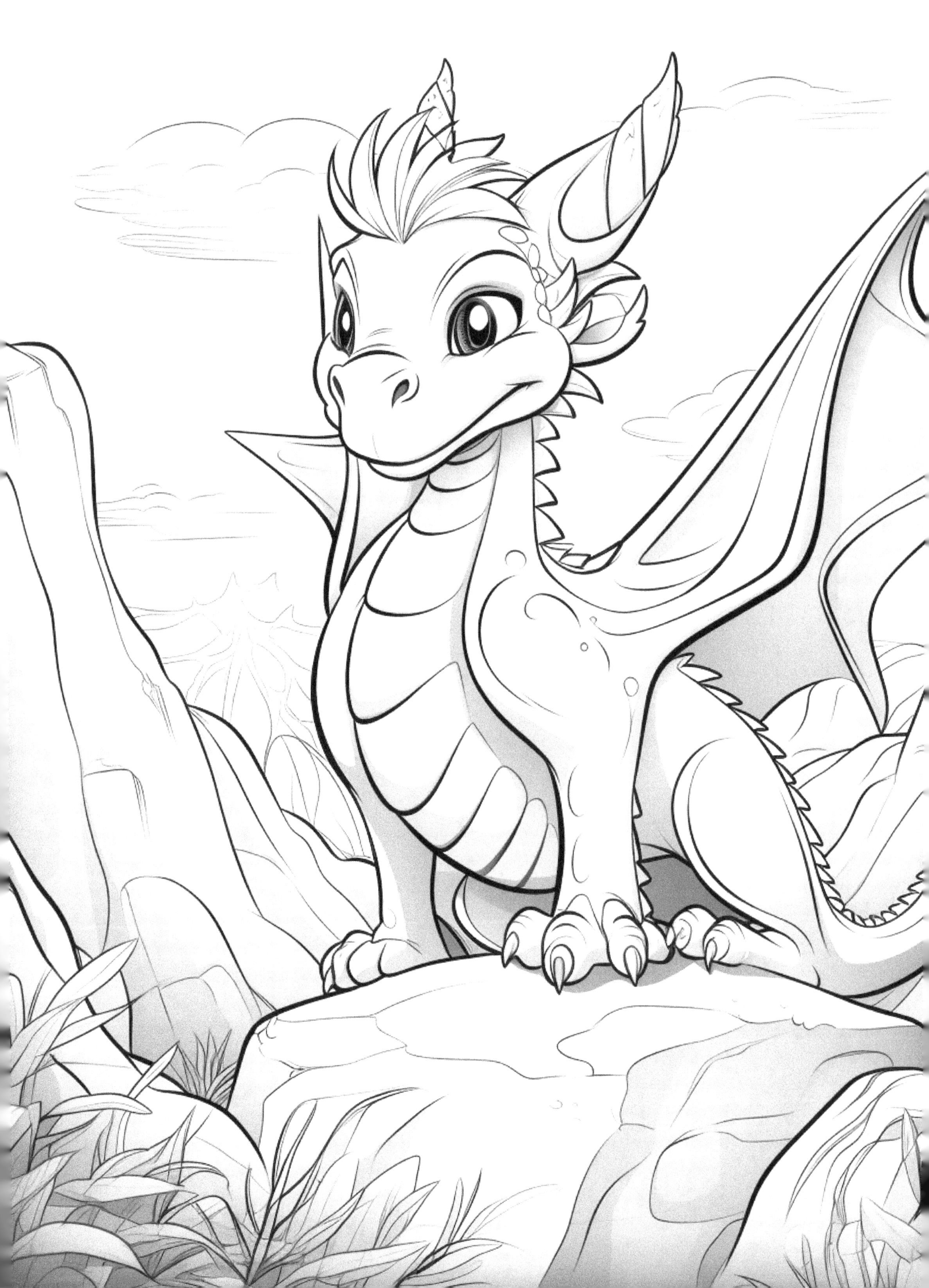

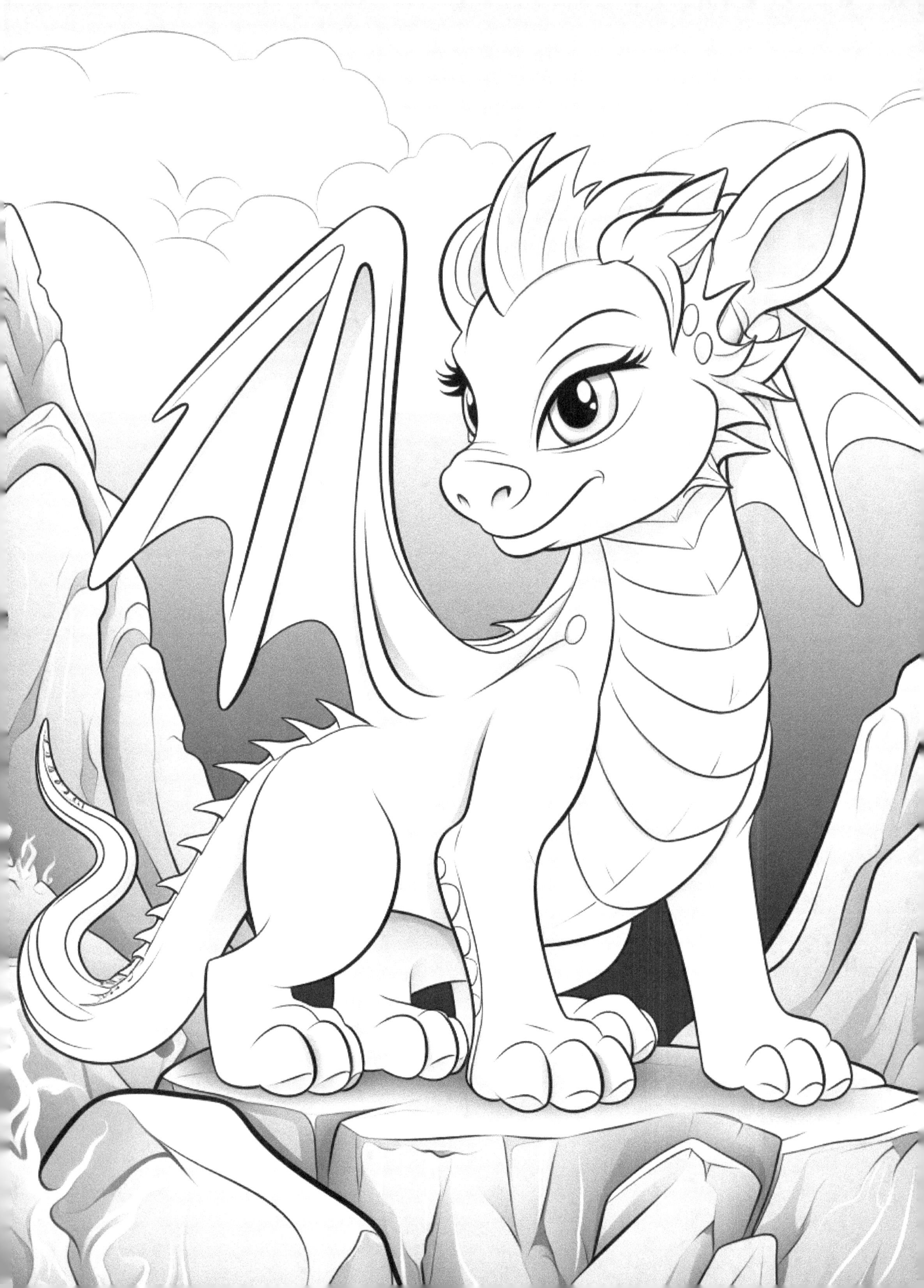

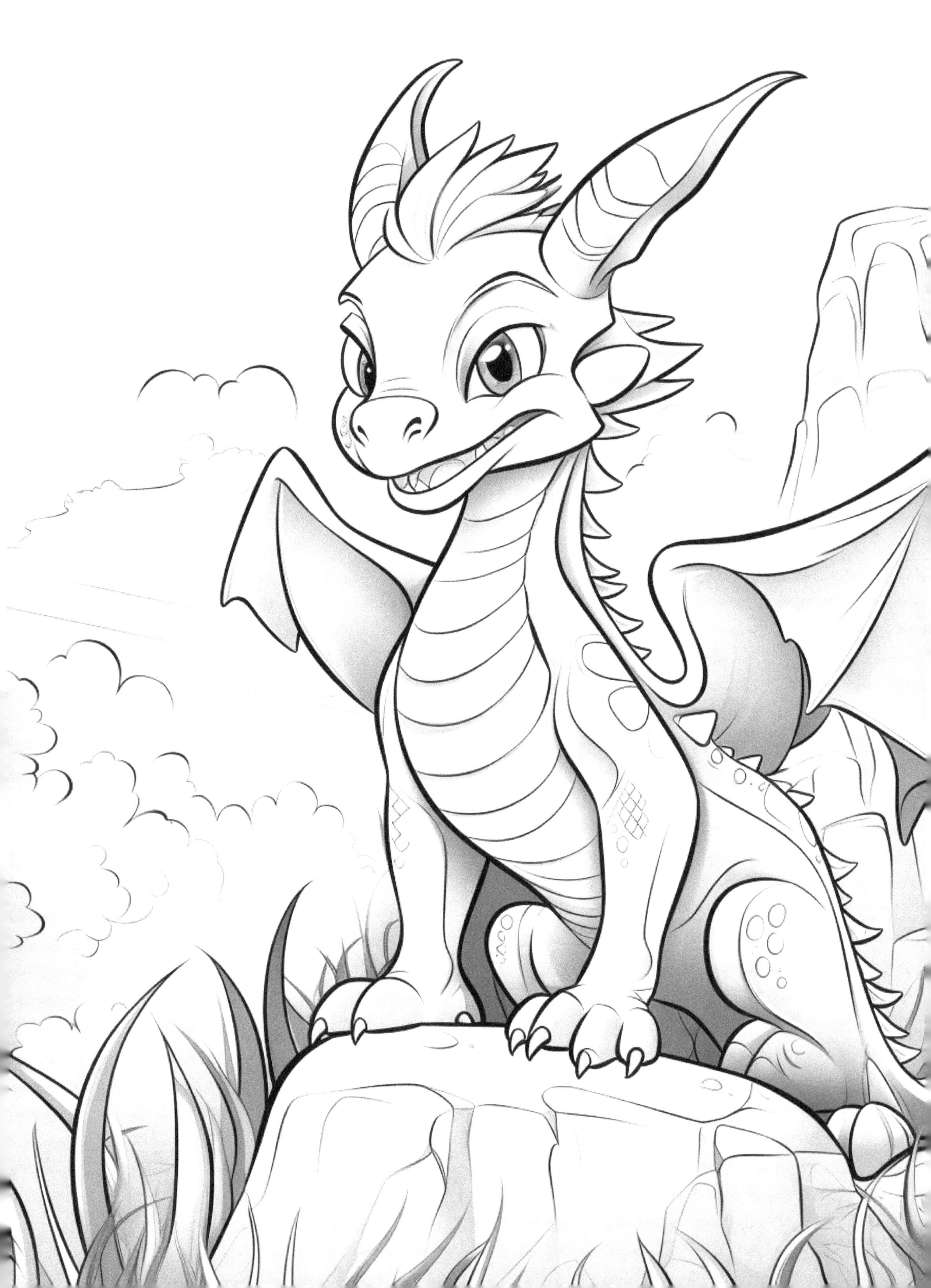

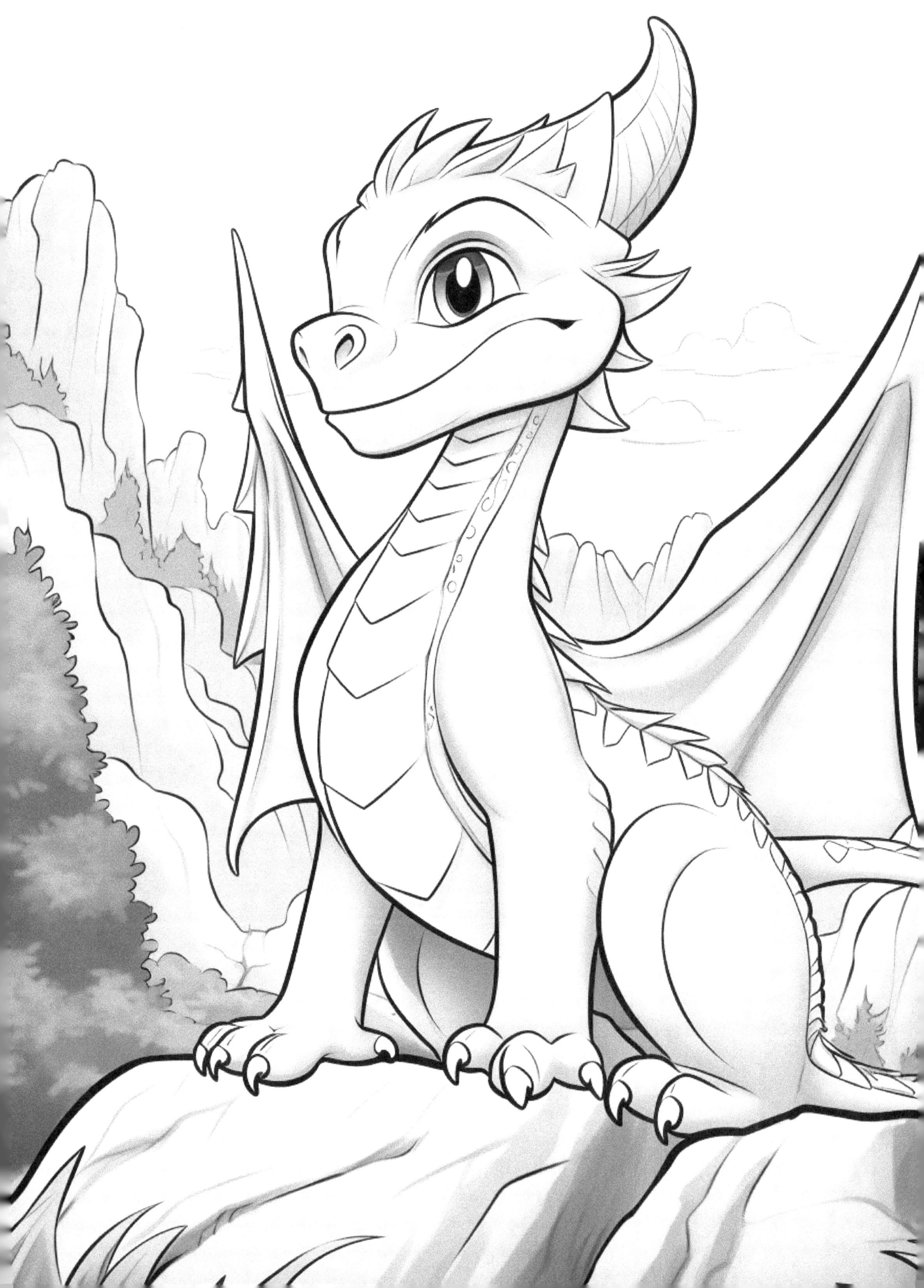

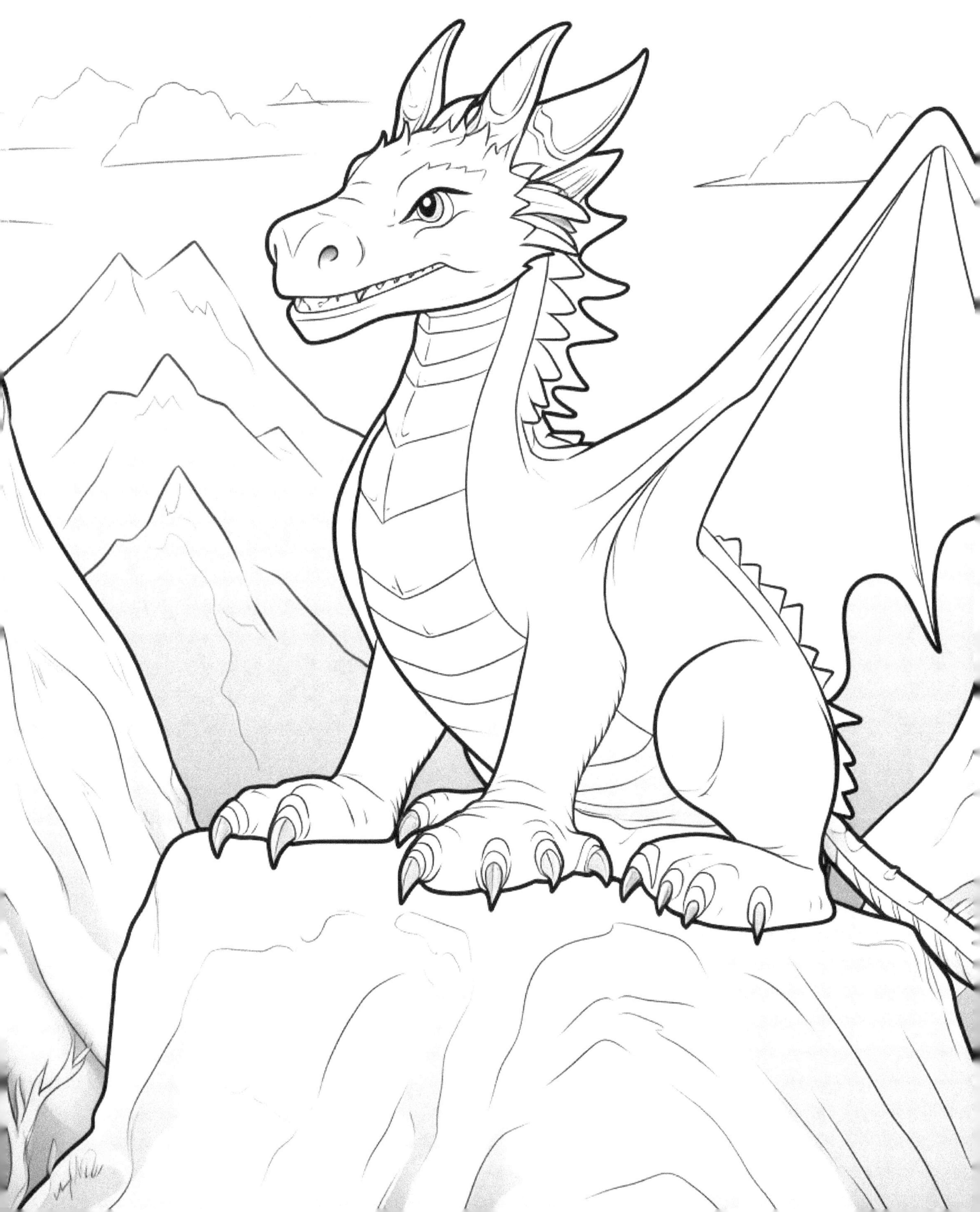